THE TERRACE GARDENER'S HANDBOOK

Drawings by Sue Gardner
Design by Page, Arbitrio & Resen

THE TERRACE GARDENER'S HANDBOOK

Raising plants on a balcony, terrace, rooftop, penthouse, or patio.

by LINDA YANG

Doubleday & Company, Inc.
Garden City, New York
1975

Library of Congress Cataloging in Publication Data

Yang, Linda.
    The terrace gardener's handbook.

    Bibliography: p. 263.
    1. Patio gardening.   2. Container gardening.
I. Title.
SB473.2.Y36   635.9'671
ISBN 0-385-09736-0
Library of Congress Catalog Card Number 74–9470

Portions of Sections 2 and 8 first appeared in the *Garden Journal,* the bimonthly publication of The New York Botanical Garden.

Haiku poems on pages 1, 21, 49, 95, 131, 185, 215, 239, 303 are translations by Harold G. Henderson from his book *An Introduction to Haiku,* Doubleday & Co., 1958. Haiku poems on pages 111, 199, 283 are translations by Harry Behn from his book *Cricket Songs,* Harcourt, Brace & World, 1964.
The poem "Pests" by Ella M. Boult is from *The Gardener's Bug Book* by Cynthia Westcott, Doubleday & Co., 1964.
Reproduction by permission of the publishers.
"Farewell! Like a bee" and "Of what use are twigs" from *Cricket Songs: Japanese Haiku,* translated and copyright © 1964 by Harry Behn. Reprinted by permission of Harcourt Brace Jovanovich, Inc.
"A spark in the sun" copyright © 1964 by Harry Behn. Reprinted from his volume, *Cricket Songs: Japanese Haiku,* by permission of Harcourt Brace Jovanovich, Inc.
Excerpts from *An Introduction to Haiku* by Harold G. Henderson. Copyright © 1958 by Harold G. Henderson. Reprinted by permission of Doubleday & Company, Inc.

Acknowledgments

Various individuals have been generous in their
willingness to help me with this work.
For their reading of parts of the manuscript and
providing me with invaluable commentary, I am
indebted to Dr. Jerry T. Walker, formerly with the
Brooklyn Botanic Garden, now Department Head,
Plant Pathology, University of Georgia; Dr.
Stephen K-M. Tim, staff member of the Brooklyn
Botanic Garden; Dr. Charles E. Kellogg, Professor
and former Head of the National Soil Survey,
USDA; and Albert P. Nordheden, ASLA, former
Senior Horticulturist of the Horticultural Society
of New York.

I wish to thank Elizabeth Scholtz, Director of the
Brooklyn Botanic Garden, and Elizabeth C. Hall,
Senior Librarian of the Horticultural Society of
New York and Associate Curator of Education
Emeritus at The New York Botanical Garden, for
their encouragement and help which dates from the
beginning of the project.

Portions of the book first appeared in the *Garden
Journal* of The New York Botanical Garden and I
am grateful to its editor, Mary E. O'Brien, for much
useful advice.

Mention must be made too of the counsel and encouragement given me by my friend Evelyn Jacobs and of the work of Executive Secretary Helen Hechter who typed (and retyped) the manuscript. Gertrude and Max Berg and their son Bob, at the Farm and Garden Nursery in Manhattan, were early sources of much information. A note of appreciation is also due Karen Van Westering, my editor at Doubleday, as well as designer Don Page of Page, Arbitrio & Resen.

Special thanks go to numerous fellow terrace gardeners for many kindnesses. Their cooperation enabled me to obtain quantities of photographs. Listed alphabetically, they include: Frank C. Baker, James W. Cherry, Mrs. Daniel G. Cone, Mrs. William E. Delehanty, Chuck Pfau, William L. Gilbertson, M. K. Goldsmith, Sue Gould, Jack Grey, Dorothy Hirshon, Mr. and Mrs. Austin Laber, Florence Lapidus, George Lax, Mary Merris, Stewart R. Mott, M. Lois Murphy, Mrs. J. Kiefer Newman, Irene O. Rosenthall, Donald Schnabel, Nancy E. Turnbull, Michael Anthony Vaccaro, R. O. Watson, Mr. and Mrs. Lorin S. Wells.

But more personal thanks are due my husband, John. I admit to frequently receiving his constructive criticism with something less than grace, but were it not for him, this book would never have been written.

Linda Yang
New York City, 1974

For my mother and father
Esther F. and Edward M. Gureasko

Contents

Foreword

Until now, most gardening literature has been directed at the home owner with a large yard and open spaces. But living conditions have changed through the years and many people in both cities and suburbs now find themselves gardening in the limited confines of a high-rise building or garden apartment, balcony, terrace, rooftop, penthouse, or patio. Gardening under these conditions, primarily in large containers, is not the same as growing plants in the ground. Thus special techniques are required whether the person is just beginning or already experienced with yard gardening.

Terrace Gardener's Handbook delves into the many situations likely to confront the owner of such a limited-size garden. It provides practical help for the terrace gardener whose problems are in some ways similar and yet quite different from his in-the-ground counterpart.

It is more than ten years since I first met Linda Yang. A practicing architect at the time, she was coming regularly to the Botanic Garden to attend our popular short courses in horticultural subjects. Fully aware that many professionals consider it to be a tremendous challenge, she had begun serious gardening on a small balcony in Manhattan. It was not long before she realized that there was a dearth of information available to gardeners laboring under such conditions. She sought help where she could find it and, where it was not available, taught herself through trial and error.

Mrs. Yang is now the mother of two and a part-time consultant with her husband's architectural firm. She has written this book in the hope that what has proved successful for her will be of use to those facing similar problems and situations. Her gardening is still confined to a Manhattan terrace, albeit a larger one now, but her practical suggestions are useful for balconies, terraces, rooftops, penthouses, and patios anywhere, in addition to small yards. As the photographs show, she very definitely refutes the widely held belief that beautiful plants cannot be grown in the city.

This most readable book is planned to function as a true workbook. Although the beginner especially will find it helpful to read through from the start, it is organized so that each chapter may be used separately as the gardener requires specific information on a subject. The extensive index and marginal reference notes will enable the reader to find his way easily to any topic covered.

As a handbook, it provides first the basics needed to set up a terrace garden. Included are explanations and detailed lists of plants and how they may best be used with regard to available growing conditions, light, and seasonal interest. Covered too is the design and arrangement of the space at hand, selection of the containers, and a step-by-step explanation of achieving a good soil mix and how to do the planting itself.

Once the garden is in place, the reader is ready for the chapters which deal with vital day-to-day tasks of keeping the plants alive and healthy. This includes discussions on proper watering throughout the year, pruning, preparing for the dormant, winter period, and dealing with the problems which arise from pests or diseases.

An especially important aspect of terrace gardening, and one which is too frequently overlooked, is maintaining the garden once it is established. Owners who have invested both time and money in their plants often become discouraged when they find their gardens beginning to decline and fade away. The typical causes of such decline, and how to prevent them, are discussed here in detail.

Appropriately, a final few words are devoted to the visiting of birds and bees, a delightful and vital part of any functioning garden no matter its size or location.

This book will be most useful to all who face the challenge of bringing the green world into their lives in the limited areas available in both cities and suburbs.

Elizabeth Scholtz
Director, Brooklyn Botanic Garden

". . . one plant in a tin can
        may be a more helpful and inspiring garden
                to some mind
than a whole acre of lawn and flowers
        may be to another . . ."

by
L. H. Bailey

from the book
*Garden Making; Suggestions for the Utilizing of
Home Grounds*

written in the year
1898

THE TERRACE
GARDENER'S
HANDBOOK

"Marvelous!" I say
as I watch, now this, now that—
and springtime goes away.
Kito

Section 1

Kinds of Plants & Where They Come From

Our country cousins with quantities of land would
have us believe that nothing can live on a terrace
or in the city. They believe this themselves. (And
sometimes we city folk marvel at our own survival.)
Yet however long man is able to live and breathe
in congested areas, so plants will be able to, too.

if man can
breathe

It is true that there are some plants which do
poorly in a polluted environment, just as there are
some people who will not thrive. But an impressive
majority, both plants and people, succeed in *adapting*
themselves with a little help from their friends.
Plants are more than just a decorative relief; every
leaf is a precious commodity. Man's life and breath
is inextricably entwined with the survival of the
plant kingdom (a point he'd do well to remember
before paving over the rest of the world). Once the
air becomes so polluted that no plants can survive,
man's days will be numbered as well . . .

In spite of limited space, the basic plant life on
terraces most assuredly can be the trees, shrubs, and

woody outdoor
types

vines which botanists call "woody," referring to the
strong texture of their bark. Some woody plants are
deciduous, which means they lose their leaves
when the cold weather comes, while others are

evergreen and retain their leaves all year. Woody plants which are tolerant of local cold weather conditions are known as "hardy" for the particular area. Buying plants which are "locally hardy" is important for every gardener. But in addition, many terrace plants will also have to be able to withstand the rigors of city life. Since, in any case, woody plants will be the most expensive part of the garden, how can one select those most likely to succeed?

Rather than wading through scientific journals, I have found that an easier (and certainly nicer) method is to purchase my plants only from a *local, reputable* dealer. "Local" for such purposes, means within about a forty-mile radius of where one lives. "Reputable" means a nurseryman with an established business of several years, selling quality stock maintained in a condition of obvious health.
You may ask: how can the beginner know what is a "condition of obvious health"?
Just take a good hard look!
An array of wilted, yellowed, pathetic-looking specimens is not the sign of stock being maintained in "obvious health." It is possible, of course, for an advanced gardener planting in the ground to rescue and resuscitate sickly plants . . . but the novice and certainly the gardener in the city is asking for trouble if he begins with anything less than an established healthy specimen.

By purchasing woody plants from a reputable dealer nearby, one is more likely to get stock which has received a good start in life. But equally important, such plants have been judged tolerant of *local* air and weather conditions by a man whose business is at stake if they prove otherwise. Note the repeated

(marginal notes)
achieving local tolerance

start with healthy stock only

use of the word "nursery."

florists are not
nurserymen
Don't confuse this word with "florist."
Your friendly neighborhood florist may be terribly
talented when it comes to flower arrangements
and he can undoubtedly supply you with lovely
hanging baskets of houseplants and colorful warm-
weather flowers (which we will discuss later on).
But rarely, if ever, are florists knowledgeable about
the hardy trees and shrubs grown on terraces in
cold climate areas. And rarer still are the ones who
stock them.

finding a
nursery
Unlike the resident of a garden apartment at the
edge of town, one of the main problems for the
mid-city dweller will be to find a nursery. Lacking
a neighbor who may also be a gardener (upstairs or
down), it is often possible to locate a source of
supply by turning to the "yellow pages" of the
telephone directory. Check such listings as
"Nurserymen," "Landscape Contractors," "Garden
Centers," "Terrace Plants," or anything similar you
may think of. If you are lucky, you will find a
dealer nearby, possibly just a taxi ride away. If there
is a Botanic Garden or Horticultural Society in the
area (see Appendix 2), write to the personnel there
as they can sometimes supply names of nurseries
for local retail purchases. Check, too, with your
Parks Department and in the spring by all means
look for weekend newspaper advertisements of such
merchants. If not found in the mid-city paper, you
can be sure they abound in the nearest suburban
journal. You may have to splurge on renting a car
for a day to reach a good supplier but the investment
is worth it.

The advantages of visiting a well-stocked nursery or
garden center becomes evident the minute you
arrive. For, let's face it, it is not possible for a

beginner to study any gardening book (this one
included) and really understand what a particular
specimen is like . . . in the flesh, so to speak. Many

why this trip
is necessary

woody plants have a particular set growth habit
which enables us to predict a general shape. But no
collection of photos or list of adjectives could hope
to depict the infinite modifications of form, color,
and growing patterns even within a single variety.
Each tree or shrub is unique, and only at the
nursery can you see subtle differences for yourself
and then purchase the very plant you like best.
I enjoy roaming about the nursery, just looking,
before making a decision about what to buy. Quite
often I arrive planning to purchase one plant and
find myself returning with something else entirely.
Contrary to the dictates of some gardening books,
there is nothing wrong with this! At most good
nurseries or garden centers, you will find the shrubs
and trees are clearly labeled with both the common
and the botanical (Latin) name. In addition,
many establishments also include informative
notes about sun requirements, water tolerance,
hardiness, and the like. There is much to be
learned simply by walking around.

The majority of the woody plants you find there

b & b stock

will be available for purchase in the form known
as "B & B." This means that the plant has been dug
out from the ground where it was growing, and the
ball of roots (the first "B") and its surrounding soil
have been wrapped in burlap (the other "B") and
tied with heavy cord. When burlap is scarce,
synthetic fabrics which look like burlap may be
used. But the important part of "B & B" stock,
where terrace gardening is concerned, is that first
"B," the ball of roots.

The next most common form you will see there

Oak leaves

container-grown plants will be "container-grown" plants. These are plants which have been grown or planted by the nurseryman in a container, often metal but also plastic, cardboard, or wood.

Trees and shrubs available in either of these forms are the only types terrace owners should consider (with very few exceptions). This is especially important for the beginner. Such plants are less apt to be affected by the "cultural shock" in their shift to new quarters since they have a generous supply of *established* roots and are surrounded and protected by the original soil in which they were grown.

Having emphasized the importance of locating and visiting a well-stocked nursery . . . and I cannot stress this point enough, I know that often it is impossible to make such visits repeatedly. So there is another way to achieve the same thing, more or less. This method is for the gardener who will take the time to acquaint himself with the trees and shrubs shown in illustrated mail-order catalogues. Much may be learned, both pleasantly and cheaply, from these little brochures which depict hundreds of plants in beautiful photographs. Mail-order nurseries advertise in newspapers or garden magazines and their booklets include brief descriptions of bloom, hardiness and light preferences of the species, and new varieties they are promoting. Naturally, they have a tendency to speak only in superlatives and I have yet to see an illustration of any tree or shrub less than absolutely perfect.

mail-order catalogues

I am a compulsive catalogue collector and reader and on cold winter nights, with the snow swirling about, these pictures of perfection haunt my dreams . . . and spring is too far away!

read carefully

But terrace owner take care. It is important to read these brochures very carefully. Sales catalogues they are . . . and sell they will . . . but what will these voluptuous catalogue trees and shrubs really be like when they arrive?

The woody plants advertised for mail order are invariably shipped in cardboard containers as "dormant bare-root stock." This means there are no leaves on the plant (dormant), there is no soil around the roots (bare root) and the specimen is extremely young. (Who but the young could make such a trip!)

dormant bare-root stock

In a garden in the ground there is nothing wrong with planting immature, dormant bare-root trees and shrubs. It is a widely practiced method and, aside from seed planting, is the least expensive way of achieving a garden. After all, even the mighty oak was once a spindly little "whip." However, while this method may be fine for a country estate or house with a twenty-year mortgage, is this what we want on our limited-size terrace or rooftop? My answer is a resounding "No!"

the twenty-year wait

With few exceptions, it will take several *years* for the pathetic specimen gasping for water in its box to recover from the shock of uprooting, the journey through the mails, and then adapt sufficiently to begin to resemble the catalogue illustration. Furthermore, as stated before, terrace life—especially in a city—is such that it is more prudent to begin with strong plants which have a well-established root system and several years of vigorous healthy growth behind them.

So, what do we do with these truly marvelous pieces of literature called mail-order catalogues? At this point, let us return for a moment to that nursery or garden center you visited. Once you have located one you like which is well stocked with healthy specimens, find out if they will also truck deliver to your building. Then take the time to establish yourself there.

I have found that nursery salespeople are generally patient and helpful . . . (the only exceptions are during those hectic Sundays in early spring). You may find that like many gardeners, they tend to be skeptical about plant life on balconies or in the city, but you can overwhelm them with your enthusiasm while you request their indulgence and help. The point is to seek out and memorize the name of one good-natured nurseryman who will also remember your name and that your "garden" is actually a terrace or balcony. Then, after studying those

glorious catalogues, and selecting a variety which
appeals to you, telephone your personal local
salesman and order it directly from him . . . B & B
or container-grown, of course! If he carries what you
saw in the mail-order catalogues, you will know it is
acceptable for your area. If not, he may be able to
suggest a similar variety which is more suitable
locally. (Some local nurseries even have their own
catalogues and you can work most conveniently
from them.)

You can then discuss important details of shape,
color, and present total height including root
ball, as well as the dimensions of its container (as
discussed in the next sections). Additional supplies
such as soil, fertilizer, etc., can also be ordered at
this time and you can sometimes arrange to have
the nursery do the planting for you. Well worth the
price, if it's a large plant.

By working this way, you will be sure of receiving a
locally tolerant plant which is a mature and
healthy specimen ready to pop into the container
and look beautiful virtually the instant you get it.

Violets

While hardy outdoor trees and shrubs may be the
basic elements of even small terraces, no summer
garden would be complete without the lush foliage
and colorful array of little flowering plants. On very
tiny balconies, these types may well be the majority

and it is not at all necessary to get them only from a "local, reliable" nursery. Provided that you check your purchase carefully for any signs of poor health and unwanted parasites, plants for such summer-only use may be bought wherever you find them. I have purchased quantities of marvelous flowers not only from my nurseryman but from the supermarket, dime store, neighborhood florist, and even from the truck vendors who appear mysteriously on city streets each spring.

Many flowers are available in individual, tiny pots, while others are in small trays where they have been grown from seed in a greenhouse. An entire lot of these trays is called a "flat."

Foremost among these summer additions are numerous species usually regarded as houseplants in cold climate zones. Some, like begonias or geraniums, flower freely, but many larger plants are used essentially for their interesting foliage. Often natives of tropical climates, they do live outside all year in their homeland. But where winters are severe gardeners have to choose between taking them indoors during the cold weather or leaving them outside to die and be purchased anew the following spring. The choice is strictly individual and depends on budget and available indoor space. In addition, you may already own several houseplants which will appreciate a summer vacation outside; they will reward you richly with vigorous new growth there. However, in cold-weather areas it is important to introduce precious houseplants to the out-of-doors very cautiously. Rare is the terrace owner who is not tempted in early spring to rush the summer and place his collection outside to make things green in a hurry, which is precisely how I lost a lovely grown-from-seed avocado one April.

houseplants
out-of-doors

don't rush
them, in or out

9

You must keep your houseplants protected from the chill breezes and strong winds they are not used to. If there is any chance of the spring weather (nights, especially) suddenly turning cold, take them back in immediately. The same principle applies in the autumn when you bring them inside. Sensitive houseplants simply should not be required to make rapid adjustments to extreme new climatic conditions, either in going out onto a cool spring terrace or coming back into a stuffy, heated apartment in late fall.

annual flowers

Along with the enticing catalogues of trees and shrubs noted previously, the terrace gardener will also be drawn to seed catalogues depicting small flowers and vegetables. Many such plants are *annuals* and differ from houseplant types in that they have a full life cycle (seed, maturity, and death) within a single year. Taking them indoors to "save them" is absolutely futile. Colorful annual flowers such as petunias or marigolds are an extremely important part of the garden. This then poses a question: should the terrace gardener start his own seeds indoors in early spring himself? If there are young children around, to whom you wish to demonstrate the miracle of life (which it is . . . and a fascinating one at that), the answer is "yes." The answer is also affirmative if you would like to have certain flowers which are relatively unusual and not easily found at garden centers. But frequently, in a small apartment, the difficulties of maintaining annuals grown from seed are such that it's expecting too much of most of us to grow many if at all.
It isn't that it's hard.
On the contrary, there are some which are quite easy to grow. The problem is really one of space and

time. A good deal more work (and mess) is involved
in growing plants indoors from seeds than the
catalogues would have you believe. Juggling soil
and leaking trays of seedlings in a tiny kitchen,
then dripping water and/or mud over your living
room rug is not the nicest way to begin the spring.
Undoubtedly it is all much easier in the larger
quarters of suburban homes. For after the seedlings
have been "thinned" (this means killing off the
extra ones) and the survivors transplanted to larger
pots for the second or third time before they may
safely be placed outside, one begins to wonder if
there isn't a better way to have summer flowers.

And of course there is. Just buy them already
grown!

By using the "ideal" conditions in the greenhouse
to condense the growing period, nurserymen enable
us to have mature annuals ready to bloom, virtually
any time we wish. Although buying these flowers
for a huge estate may be no small expense, their cost
for a terrace is so minimal that it is unnecessary to
subject ourselves to growing them indoors from
seed.

So you may ask: why not sow the seeds outside in
the first place?

A valid question to be sure. And the answer is:
because it generally takes too long. Seeds sown
outdoors will not begin to sprout until the moisture
condition and the ground and air temperatures are
acceptable. This means that if the spring is cool,
late, or dry, you may not see your beautiful flowers
until well into summer, or even later.

This is certainly not what I want.

How much better to buy them from commercial
sources when you want them, just as they are about
to burst into bloom in just the right color and size.

On the other hand, there is nothing more delightful or ego-satisfying than using fresh herbs or vegetables from your own little garden. (And with food costs increasing, a few city terrace owners now have nothing *but* edible plants.)

home-grown edibles are worthwhile

Some of the more common food plants such as tomatoes, parsley, and basil may be found at garden centers already started by nurserymen. But most others are not. This means if you'd like to have them, you *must* grow them from seed yourself. And this is a different matter.

Since you will not be growing vegetables or herbs for their marvelous good looks (very few are anything to admire in that sense) you really won't miss their presence in your early summer garden. For this reason it is entirely possible to sow the seeds directly in your containers outside, waiting till the preferred conditions are right. Directions about safe planting times, required light, etc., are listed on the seed packets themselves (usually with a glorious picture of what you'll have if successful). If you decide to start your seed planting indoors, it's a good idea to begin a little later than the package suggests for your locale. I've found that this delay saves on the number of indoor transplantings needed before it's warm enough to safely move the seedlings outside.

vegetables and herbs

Vegetable and herb seed packages can be found virtually anywhere but for a really wide selection it is best to write for the brochure of one of the major suppliers. A few of these are:

> Parks Seed Co.
> Greenwood, South Carolina 29646

> W. Atlee Burpee Co.
> P. O. Box 6929
> Philadelphia, Pennsylvania 19132
> also Riverside, California 92502

Stokes Seeds, Inc.
P. O. Box 15
Buffalo, New York 14205

Burgess Seed & Plant Co.
Galesburg, Michigan 49053

perennials

The final category of smaller plant types are the *perennials*. Taylor's Encyclopedia defines a perennial as a "nearly ever-living plant." Technically of course this includes trees, shrubs, and many houseplants. But when gardeners speak of perennials they *mean* outdoor plants like iris, day lilies, or gladiolas, which return to flower year after year even though they may die back completely each winter.

Perennials are the mainstay of many large gardens and with good reason, too . . . they need not be replaced each year and at one season or another can be counted upon to do the right thing. But they are not like flowering annuals which add color throughout the summer and then are removed and discarded. Most perennials have a comparatively short flowering period, spend the rest of their time coming up or dying down, and have no interesting winter form.

Thus, for terrace gardens where planting space is at a premium, perennials are not especially useful additions. Furthermore, they get in the way when it's time to cultivate the soil in the tubs (a very important point discussed later). A few perennials are fine if there is also sufficient room for annuals, trees, and shrubs. But I really feel that if your large container space is limited, it should not be wasted on perennials. (Unless, of course, you treat them as if they were annuals and get rid of them when they have finished blooming.)

However, if you happen to like a particular one or do have lots of room, stick to those perennials which

if growing
space is

are found in that "local, reliable" nursery where you buy your woody trees and shrubs. The same principles are involved. The roots of such plants must be winter hardy for your particular area. And again, you have a better chance for success if they are planted as mature established specimens.

spring bulbs

Although the same space-consuming disadvantages of perennials apply to flowering bulbs, the spring-blooming ones like hyacinths, tulips, or crocuses are such gems they are worth every inch. Planted in late fall, spring-flowering bulbs of good quality may be purchased from reputable mail-order houses, as well as from nurseries. Many gardeners leave their stronger spring bulbs in the ground all year, planting their annuals right over them. But our containers are so limited in size and soil cultivation so important that I feel it is a better practice, and not at all difficult, to dig them up once their leaves have died completely and store them away until the next fall. I prefer to plant only bulbs which are freshly

planting anew
or using the
old

purchased each year. But if you wish to replant the old ones, buy only varieties which are recognized as strong repeaters. Many types of highly hybridized tulips, for example, are quite weak and cannot be expected to repeat their bloom. (However, this is usually not true of those known as "botanicals.") Although spring bulbs must be planted in the fall when we look forward to our own period of rest, they are well worth the added time and trouble. After a long and dreary winter, the sight of their intense colors is truly among the most glorious of gardening experiences.

There are times when the terrace gardener is out in the country and discovers an interesting plant he'd like to have at home. There are several reasons why

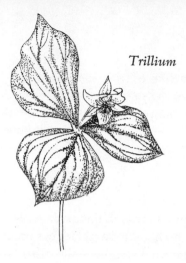

Trillium

he must resist the temptation to yank it out of the
ground and make off with it. Aside from the fact
that he has not asked permission of the owner of
the land and is removing something which may not
be available for his taking . . . there is another
question to be asked. That is: will the plant survive
such an ordeal or is he really only killing it by this
act?

As discussed earlier, plants bought as nursery-grown
stock have a root system which is intact, healthy,
and well established because the nurseryman
developed it as such. This is not true for a plant
which is growing wild. Having all of the
surrounding acreage in which to grow, sideways as
well as down it does just that. No matter how
carefully you may think you are digging it up,
chances are you cannot preserve enough of the root
system to enable the plant to stand the shock of
uprooting, transplanting, and then the change to
the city. It's like attempting to tame a wild animal
which has always been free.

If you really fall in love with a wild plant (and it
does happen often) and you don't know what it is
(and that too happens, just as often), CAREFULLY
cut off a portion of *one* small branch with enough

15

leaves, flowers, or fruit, so that a proper identification can be made later. Spread the specimen between several thicknesses of newspaper and it will be preserved. Since it is impossible to identify plants from verbal descriptions only, take it to your nurseryman who may or may not be able to identify it, or mail it to the nearest expert for help (see Appendix 2).

If you send it through the mail, reinforce the parcel sufficiently that breakage does not occur. The New York Botanical Garden, one institution having a plant identification service, requests that as much additional information as possible, based on your observations, be supplied. But no matter where you take or send it, be sure to list:

submitting
plants
for
identification

1. Growing habit of the plant
   (tree, shrub, creeper, twiner, etc.)
2. Habitat
   (was it found growing in a
   vacant lot, by the road, forest, etc.)
3. General light conditions
   (full sun, etc.)
4. Time of year of collection
5. Original color of leaves, flower,
   or fruit

And for goodness' sake, don't forget to include your own name and address; a self-addressed, stamped envelope is also much appreciated!

Once the specimen has been identified, you can proceed to buy it container-grown or B & B, if it's available in your locale. If it's not available locally, but you must have it anyway, by all means track it down and buy it wherever it may be found.

Mail-order houses are useful for this purpose and if you regard the entire venture as an experiment, you will not be upset if it doesn't work. At least you will know that you have left the original plant in the wild, where it belongs and is still alive.

EVEN THE
TINIEST
BALCONY CAN
HAVE AN
ARRAY OF
COLORFUL
PETUNIAS AND
TROPICAL
HOUSEPLANTS

ANNUALS AND
HOUSEPLANTS
TURN AN
ENLARGED
FIRE ESCAPE
INTO A SMALL
SUMMER
GARDEN

NURSERYMEN
DELIVERING
A SMALL
DORMANT B & B
TREE

TAKING
A RIDE
IN THE
ELEVATOR

NURSERY
TRAYS
OF PORTULACA
SEEDLINGS
READY FOR
PLANTING

PARSLEY
SEEDLINGS
REMAIN
INDOORS
UNTIL SPRING
IS HERE TO STAY

HOME-GROWN
TOMATOES
RIPEN ON THE
VINE, NOT IN
A WAREHOUSE

SOME OF
THESE
SUNFLOWER
SEEDS WILL BE
EATEN, SOME
SAVED FOR
PLANTING
NEXT YEAR

CONSIDER
YOUR TERRACE
AS SEEN FROM
INSIDE, ALL
YEAR LONG

IN THE FALL,
VIRGINIA
CREEPER ON
THE FENCE
OUTSIDE IS A
BLAZE OF
COLOR

The winds that blow—
ask them, which leaf of the tree
will be next to go!
Soseki

Section 2

A Little Planning

How often I've heard the lament "I have no room
for any plants."
Well, if it's possible to walk outside and turn around
again, it's possible to find a spot not only for summer
flowers but for a small tree or shrub too. The terrace
does not exist which cannot have at least one little
tree . . . . and often more than one can be
accommodated as well. Therefore, I refuse to accept
the plea of "no room" from anyone. (Laziness is
probably closer to the truth.)

no room for
trees or
shrubs?

Now a terrace is not a large country estate and one
needn't approach its planning as if it were. Estate
gardeners may plant a tree or shrub in the ground
and that is the end of that. But terrace gardening is
unique in that the existence and future location of
any plant may at *any* time be subject to change.
No estate gardener in his right mind expects to
move his plants about his property. Yet with trees
and shrubs in containers, the terrace gardener may
do so every spring or fall if he wishes.
But more important, terrace plants are not static
pieces of furniture. They are living, growing (and
sometimes dying) things which change throughout
the seasons and the years. No amount of "planning

a terrace is not
a country
estate

ahead" will change this basic fact. Thus, I feel it's

a flexible
attitude first

best to establish a flexible attitude toward both the planning and the plants and then remember to try to maintain this outlook. Which means, among other things, departing from the books and magazines which exhort gardeners to "carefully plan ahead."

This is not to say the terrace gardener won't do some planning . . . only that it's unnecessary to plot everything in detail and rigidly adhere to these ideas! Terrace plans *can* be permitted to *grow and change,* just as the plants themselves will, over a period of time.

getting to
know your
own conditions

No matter the size (and whether or not you intend to plan and maintain it entirely alone), it's important first to understand your own special conditions. You may have "seen" your terrace before, but chances are you haven't really *looked* at it. So before doing anything else, one must make several visits outside for the express purpose of observation. And right now is as good a time as any to eliminate all sit-at-the-desk routines, because gardening is not

get thee
outside

office work. Plan to make your visits not only on several different days but at different times of the day as well. Even for the most minute garden, it's wise to bring along a pen and something stiff on which to note observations which will be important later on. (For this, I'm a shirt-cardboard and shoebox-top fan myself.)

Unless the area is quite tiny, the first order of business will be to make a simple diagram of the shape of your floor. It's not at all difficult to measure and write down two of the "basic statistics," namely,

your basic
statistics

the narrowest and widest dimensions. Don't panic if it's not an easy shape like a rectangle, but is an L or U or something on that order. It's just the basic form you're after.

Rose twig

Now in any garden there are numerous small climatic conditions known as *microclimates* which profoundly affect the planting success. In the city especially, astronomy and a working knowledge of the compass are useless since these conditions often appear to defy rules of logic and science. But

fortunately, they are easily found by direct
observation. For example, just because the building
agent told you the apartment "faces south," don't
assume you will have blinding sunlight all over
your garden all day long. If another structure
blocks any portion of your terrace, then the light
there is no longer the "south" to which gardening
books refer. Therefore, note the duration and
location of the sunlight you *actually* see. Since
some plants are happy with a few hours of gentle
light, but will resent strong midday sun (and vice
versa), note not only where and for how long the
light is on the terrace but also the time of day it
appears there.

actual sunlight

Nature is kind to apartment dwellers, for in the
summer the sun shifts to a higher position in the sky
and rises and sets more to the north. This means
that in spite of your "exposure" or surrounding tall
buildings, it's likely you will find you have more
light during the growing period than you observed
at other times of the year. However, do not despair
if you discover you are in shade most of the time.
Whole forests manage beautifully like this and if
you are aware of your conditions from the
beginning, I promise you, your garden can be
beautiful too.

reflected light

Useful light for some plants will also include
reflections. In the summer, several hours after
sunrise I find the west side of my terrace bathed in
brilliant morning light. It is from the rising sun all
right, but it is being *reflected* onto my terrace by an
adjacent building. The shiny windows and glazed
white brick wall of this helpful neighbor is the
unexpected source of bright morning light.

In addition to affecting available light, the
chasm-like alleys between buildings (especially tall

24

ones) often produce unusual wind and temperature conditions. Microclimates surrounding suburban gardens in Long Island were discussed by nurseryman Andre Viette, in a lecture to the Horticultural Society of New York. He had observed temperature differences of as much as 10° Fahrenheit within several *feet* of each other. If that is typical for large suburban gardens, consider how such conditions abound in small city ones.

winds

Wind strength, direction, and location can vary widely even on the same terrace . . . and it's useful to know this in advance. Quite often it's possible to avoid planting a sensitive specimen in a high wind pocket simply by placing it on the other side of the terrace or just a few feet away.
Fortunately, many plants, once established, manage to adapt to wind. They may have their flowers blown away sooner, but the petals can still be enjoyed while they're on the floor.
Some winds produce peculiar results.
For example, in New York City, the strongest winds reputedly blow from the northeast. But the conditions surrounding my terrace frequently cause them to reverse and my plants are subject instead to winds which blow from the south. As a result, some of my taller trees actually lean away from the sun and to the north.

winds which
reverse

One summer before I realized that my winds reversed, the children's plastic swimming pool mysteriously disappeared. A bad storm had hit, which the weatherman had said was coming from the west. Since my terrace is blocked on that side by another taller building, I assumed I had everything secured until I realized the pool was gone. After a week of being utterly mystified, I summoned the courage to peer down many stories over that west-side fence. Sure enough, there was the children's pool lying in a ground-level garden below.

Becoming acquainted with your terrace also means knowing all your views. Breath-taking skyscapes, if you are lucky to have them, should be noted of course. But just as important are unattractive sights and rare indeed is the terrace which does not have some unwanted view.

views, wanted and unwanted

You may discover an ugly plastic divider, oppressive water tower, overwhelming brick wall, a too-near neighbor, or even a frightening sheer drop.
Note whatever you see that you don't like and where it occurs. In addition, do not overlook the views of the terrace itself as *seen from within* your own apartment. Never mind that it may not be outside the living room, because these "framed pictures" wherever they occur are extremely important, as we shall see shortly.

Some terrace owners may decide to install an awning, while newer apartment buildings have balconies one above the other in tiers. Thus some prospective gardeners will look up and find a ceiling instead of the sky.

a roof overhead?

If this is your situation, remember that this roof will be a problem only if you try to ignore it! By accepting its presence you can observe how it affects your terrace with regard to light and growing conditions. For example, a roof or awning will reduce or completely eliminate your rainwater supply. While no good gardener relies only on heaven, a gardener with a roof must be especially prepared to deal with this.
Don't feel disheartened, however, as there is one major advantage to having a ceiling over your head. You can HANG things from it.
And for tiny gardens, this should not be ignored.

If you find such a roof, you may be able to increase your reflected light by painting the underside white. This is hardly equal to the open sky but it will be better than before. (It will look better, too.) If you're nervous about climbing up high to do the job, get a roller with a long extension handle, and it's not difficult at all.

Some inventive balcony owners with concrete roofs have painted them with designs, rather than a solid color. Still others I've seen have chosen to attach canvas or vinyl fabric to the ceiling surface, thus giving the appearance of an "awning" overhead.

Clematis flowers

While I'm on the subject of roofs and height, if you live on a high floor it's worthwhile, too, to take a look at and measure your elevator. I once had a dreadful experience with my building's superintendent because of this. A tree I had ordered from a distant nursery was delivered when I was not at home. The super took one look at it, declared it would "never fit in the elevator" and made the nurserymen take it back!

the elevator

The unkind remarks I subsequently made about him are not fit to print, for not only is the elevator's diagonal dimension a good deal longer than its height, but there is also a small *top panel* which can be opened for emergencies. These panels may not have been planned with trees in mind, but determined gardeners certainly can make use of them.

Then, too, trees are flexible to a certain extent and I feel that a few bent or even broken branches are a small price to pay for a fine, mature specimen.

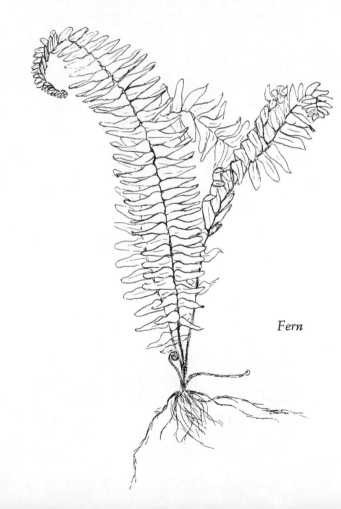

Fern

Once you know a bit about your terrace conditions, it's possible to outline some first ideas.

chalking up some ideas
There are many ways to go about this, but my favorite and the way I continue to work is especially helpful for the beginner, unfamiliar with names or types. Before I worry about selecting a specific plant, I start by thinking of planting areas and plant forms in *general* as they relate to the conditions. The easiest way to do this is by using *chalk and drawing right on the terrace floor* (Here's one advantage to not having a lawn.)

creating "views"
Representing container areas by circles and/or rectangles no less than about one foot in diameter (but larger if there's room), begin by blocking out some planting spots just outside of your *windows*. The idea first is to try to imagine little "garden views" of the larger plant forms (trees, shrubs or vines) to be seen from inside all year long. Place these groups either right next to the building or farther away near the outside wall . . . and both if possible. On tiny balconies, be sure to make the most of your corners and far ends. If you are lucky and found that you have an interesting view beyond, place your chalk-drawn container areas so that the plants eventually frame the view. Otherwise, locate them so they help block or at least minimize what you'd rather not see.

a scene for all seasons
As you form these inside-looking-out pictures, try to think of what happens in nature at different times of the year. For unlike other apartment dwellers, we with outdoor plants are privileged in our sense of the changing seasons . . . opening buds and flowers in the spring, rich foliage in the summer, colored leaves and berries in the autumn, and bare branches or snow-covered evergreens in the winter. Our trees and shrubs may not achieve the extreme hues or magnificent proportions of those planted in

the ground, but each season does provide us with exciting changes. Especially when seen from inside, all year long.

ideas for
narrow spots

Finding enough growing room for plants, while keeping enough living room for humans, is often a major terrace dilemma. Sometimes this can be accomplished by planning to use trees and shrubs which are naturally narrow in their growth habit. But another way is to make use of vines and climbers. Such plants are also good for helping minimize (or cover) your unattractive objects or views.

Some vines and climbers will cling by themselves to walls or railings while others will need some help, especially in windy spots. The trellis is a classic method of climber support, but plants will be equally happy with chicken wire or mesh, plastic ties or hooks or nails strung with coated wire. These are all easily available from dime stores as well as from hardware or electrical suppliers.

One especially useful product I have come across is the "Wayward Vine Support." It consists of a small round piece of cement with a bendable metal extension. The round part is glued to the wall with a special waterproof adhesive and once it is dry the metal part may be bent so that it holds the vine or branch in place. This product is available at many garden centers, but if you can't find it, write the distributor: Louis S. Mauger, Inc., P. O. Box 801, New Canaan, Connecticut 06840.

espaliered
plants

Sometimes it is possible to find "narrow" growing plants which are so unique they immediately attract attention and are useful for a multitude of reasons. One such group of trees and shrubs are those which have been *espaliered,* that is, trained to grow in a symmetrical design, but flattened against a special form.

The history of the espalier dates back to ancient days, but the technique is still practiced in European orchards to save space. Once used mostly for edible, fruiting plants, many nursery-trained espalier trees and shrubs can now be bought for small garden use. The formal espalier is typically a definite symmetrical design. However, the idea of using *any* plant which has branches which are flexible enough to train flat against the wall is extremely helpful for narrow areas. (And of course another way to gain space is to weave branches out past the railing and over the street. Every inch counts!)

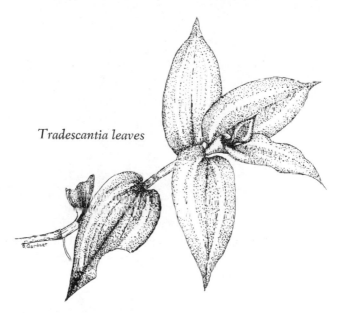

Tradescantia leaves

In addition to the width restriction, you may have found you are also going to have to cope with a limited height of plant (that "roof" or an awning). Contrary to what you may think at first, this doesn't mean you won't be able to have a tree. It just has to be the right kind of tree.

coping with
height limits

Among the useful types for this are ones with *weeping* forms. And there are many varieties of flowering deciduous trees and shrubs as well as some evergreens which grow in this manner. Because these graceful plants "grow down" rather than up, they solve the height problem while adding more than their share of interest.

Also useful for the limited height spots are the unusual *dwarf* varieties of many trees and shrubs. Again, don't worry about specific plant names now, just be sure you have envisioned a general shape, height, and width and chalked up its approximate location.

Primrose

If you discovered earlier that your terrace or a portion thereof is subject to such extreme winds that it's altogether unbearable, then it's worthwhile now to plan on trying to minimize the force of these winds.

minimizing winds

One of the best ways to do this is to create a barrier of fairly tall, wind-tolerant plants located on the side the wind appears to be coming from. If the direction is not consistent, or if you're not sure which way blows worse, chalk up the place for these plants where they will also be useful for other functions, such as blocking an unwanted view or sheer drop. The tall, finger-like branches of the plants in this "wall" help break the wind's force while causing an up and over air stream. The more tall plants you then add throughout the terrace, the more you will succeed in mitigating the wind's force, or actually altering your microclimatic condition. Smaller and less tolerant varieties may then be safely planted as well. You will not succeed in stopping it altogether, but you may bring the wind under control enough to make the garden more pleasant for both humans and other plants. However, be sure to plan on giving your "windbreakers" room enough for the largest containers possible; their roots will need every bit of anchoring space you can spare.

At this point if you can still walk past all your chalk scrawlings on the floor, you will have an inkling of both the approximate number and position of the *major* planting areas you can have. So now it's

an illusion of spaciousness

time to take stock of the *spaces* created. Your plants will not all be the same size and shape (I hope), so your planting areas and containers need not be either. Keeping in mind that planting tubs don't have to be lined up like soldiers against a wall, remember that a terrace is not a "super-highway." It should be a leisurely, meandering, "parkway," no matter how tiny or narrow the space. For the small patio as well as the huge rooftop, the principle is still the same; larger groupings of plants or containers *randomly* alternated with smaller, differently shaped ones create a more interesting appearance as well as the illusion of space. (And none of us can have too much of either of these.) The "bowling alley" feeling on especially long and narrow terraces is relieved when a variety of different spaces follow each other in sequence.

Once you have the basic garden consisting of hardy outdoor trees, shrubs, and vines outlined, it's easy next to plan for the smaller plants. And on very tiny balconies these will be a majority.
In the city especially, flowering annuals, houseplants, vegetables, and herbs make gardening a delight. But unless yours is a tropical climate, most of these plants will adorn the terrace garden only during the warm summer months. For these plants, an even more flexible planning approach is possible since they may be treated quite casually: left standing here and there on the floor in their own small containers or grouped together in long window boxes along the railing or wall. Still others may be hung in baskets from a "roof" above, awning frame, or even from the building wall itself.
One method which I favor especially is to plant the small warm weather plants in the same large containers with my trees, shrubs, and vines. A few inches of space is all the little ones require and the big ones don't mind at all. You need not worry about breaking a few of the larger plants' roots when you do this, either.
In other words, wherever warm weather plants can possibly be made to fit, they should be. And this is true even for the smaller vegetables and herbs. Aside from making the most of our limited spaces, interplanting edible plants among flowers and other nonedibles is considered by many to be the only way to run a real garden. But I was reminded of another of its advantages by Kate Rogers, who helps with the children's section of the Brooklyn Botanic Garden: that of pest control. This subject is discussed later but suffice it to say now

the smaller plants

small plants in tubs with big ones

mixing edibles with nonedibles

that some plants repel certain insects while others attract them. Interplanting of this sort actually helps to control pests.

However, in my case, my family is happiest with a dense "jungle-like" profusion of plant life. Thanks to these many smaller plants, by the end of the summer my terrace certainly looks that way.

Sunflower

storing supplies

Outside storage space for gardening tools and supplies is extremely useful and very desirable. But unless you've lots of room, you must be clever about finding leftover corners for it. For balconies which are limited in area, it is possible to buy or build a low storage unit, like a "deacon's bench," which can double as a support for small plants or a place to sit. Garden centers and mail-order houses feature miniature tool sheds which can be used when space is not at a premium. But whether you get a small bench or a large tool shed, make sure that it's constructed of a durable, weatherproof material even if you "finish" it yourself. It's rather bothersome to find you have a rusty, decaying heap after only two or three years.

In any case, try to find or devise some storage spot outside, or else be prepared to find it inside.

In addition to gardening, terraces serve a variety of other uses for their owners. Think over what you might like and, if the space is particularly large, the best location for the activity. For example, evening dining is especially exhilarating outside and more than one terrace owner has breakfast or lunch there as well.

furniture

Chairs and tables for outside must be weatherproof if you expect to leave them there all year. Redwood furniture survives well but often is too large for smaller gardens. Wrought iron is quite durable, takes less space, and can be spray-painted if black doesn't appeal to you. Rattan is another favorite, but if left outside in midcity, often becomes impossibly dirty.

If you're short on space for permanent furniture, you can find lightweight folding chairs and tables of aluminum. My first terrace was quite small and these were useful indeed. And finally, furniture of durable plastic is also available now, often in a variety of cheerful colors. Late summer or early fall, by the way, is the best time to get good buys on outdoor furniture.

On larger terraces there may be room for additional items such as playhouses, sundials, birdbaths, or garden sculpture. You probably won't find just what you like immediately, but when you do, locate those you really want to see all year in a spot where you will really see them . . . from inside.

If you wish to have a plastic swimming pool for children, resist the temptation to get a large one. A gallon of water weighs about nine pounds and in such quantity is extremely heavy. While the terrace might not collapse completely, more cracks are *not* what's needed either.

Some gardeners enjoy looking at their gardens at night and supply centers carry weatherproof lights which may be left outside all year. However,

lighting running electrical cables to the right spot for hookup can be something of a feat on a large terrace. The nicest and certainly most dramatic method of lighting plants at night is from the *bottom up* and not the other way around. Some terrace gardeners install additional downlights in order to work outside in the evening. But since the sun sets quite late during the summer, I feel that additional lighting for this purpose alone is not really needed.

Sometimes, despite the most clever screen of plants, a complete blocking of an area is necessary after all.

fences which For this there are many practical as well as
cover decorative styles of fencing available.
completely "Stockade"-style cedar stakes and wood pickets are my favorites but there are other types of fences or latticework to be found in garden centers as well as in hardware or department stores. Sometimes you can devise one yourself. I found that bamboo shades, for example, when turned on their side, are a practical and inexpensive screen. While not windproof, they will cover up a multitude of sins. Stained wood planks placed in some interesting pattern of alternate wide and narrow strips are another possibility for the do-it-yourselfer.

fences which If the terrace is on a high floor and must be made
only protect safe for climbing children (or adults with fear of heights) but you don't want to block the view,

many patterns of "chicken wire" are also available. There are thin-gauge types which are just as strong but not as awful-looking as the usual school-playground variety. In any case, wherever possible, also think of these screens as potential backgrounds for plant life.

As you can see, if there's room for *you* on your terrace, there's room for quite a few plants too. The time you spend making an effort to become acquainted with your conditions and thinking about some of the plant forms which might be suitable will enable you to be prepared to deal with many aspects as time goes on. And this includes being able to make use of numerous fine gardening books which weren't written with you in mind.
You're now ready for the detailed lists in the next chapter.

STATELY
PYRAMIDAL
JUNIPERS ARE
PRACTICAL
ACCENT
PLANTS

FOR SPOTS
WITH HEIGHT
LIMITATIONS,
WEEPING
PLANTS LIKE
THIS
FLOWERING
PEA TREE ARE
EXTREMELY
USEFUL

A SUMMER
WINDOW
LOOKS OUT ON
FLOWERING
ROSE
STANDARDS
AND PANSIES

MANY PLANTS
CAN BE
TRAINED TO
GROW "FLAT."
CUCUMBERS
ARE NO
EXCEPTION

NAILS AND
COATED
WIRE HELP
A TWINING
VINE

A SNOWY DAY
AND
BROADLEAVED
EVERGREENS
ARE OUTSIDE

THIS SMALL ESPALIERED
JUNIPER (STILL
IN ITS NURSERY
CONTAINER)
WILL TAKE A
MINIMUM OF SPACE

EVEN A LARGE
ESPALIERED
PEAR TREE
OCCUPIES
HARDLY ANY
ROOM AT ALL

A FENCE OF WHITE PLANKS IS BOTH ATTRACTIVE AND A GOOD BACKGROUND FOR THIS CLIMBING EVERGREEN EUONYMUS

THIS WALL LAMP ALSO PROVIDES SUPPORT FOR CLIMBING ROSES

A STONE
CHERUB CON-
TEMPLATES
SOME LARGE
CALADIUM
LEAVES

THE TREES
AND SHRUBS
CREATE A
FEELING OF
ENCLOSURE
AND
PRIVACY

DINING AL
FRESCO
SURROUNDED
BY VINES AND
SUMMER
FLOWERS

A SMALL
HOMEMADE
STORAGE
CABINET IS
TUCKED
BEHIND THE
PLANTS

HONEYSUCKLE CLIMBS A
CHIMNEY BEHIND A
HOMEMADE PICNIC TABLE.
SNAPDRAGON FLOWERS ARE
IN THE CONTAINER ON
THE FLOOR

A CLIMBING
HYDRANGEA IS
AIDED BY THE
"WAYWARD
VINE SUPPORT"

A LARGE
STORAGE
CABINET FITS
A "SPARE"
CORNER

WHEN OPEN, IT'S A
STORAGE UNIT, WHEN
CLOSED, IT'S A SEAT; A
"DEACON'S BENCH"
IS A USEFUL
BALCONY ADDITION

45

A WOOD FENCE PROVIDES A BACKDROP FOR A CRAB-APPLE TREE AS WELL AS YEAR-ROUND PATTERNS AND PRIVACY

FLUFFY GERANIUMS IN FRONT OF A WHITE PICKET FENCE WHICH HIDES A SHEER DROP

A "DUBOIS"
OR STOCKADE
FENCE
OBSCURES AN
UNDESIRABLE
VIEW WHILE
SUPPORTING
A WALL OF
INFORMALLY
ESPALIERED
FIRETHORN

THIS HOME-
MADE FENCE
OF
ALTERNATING
WOOD PLANKS
ALSO
SUPPORTS A
WISTERIA
VINE

FINE WIRE
MESH HELPS
A VIRGINIA
CREEPER
CLIMB THE
WALL

THE BLACK
PINE IS
TOLERANT OF
HIGH WIND
CONDITIONS

A morning-glory vine,
all blossoming, has thatched
this hut of mine.

Issa

Section 3

Narrowing the Choices; Names of Useful Plants

Having luxuriated for a few moments now in the imagined foliage on the chalk-filled terrace, the novice may suddenly realize that he doesn't know the name of a single plant to buy! After all, knowledge of these names has little relevance to normal apartment living . . . and few and far between are those of us who know one plant from another in the beginning. So you may be surprised to discover at this point that having read the preceding sections you really DO know a great deal more about the plants for your terrace than you suspect. And it's possible to make a list of descriptive words and required traits which

some key
questions to
answer

characterize those plants which are most suitable. For *each chalk area on your floor* you can now respond to five key questions (jotting ideas down if you wish on the cardboard drawing):

1. *WHAT LIGHT*
   TOLERANCE WILL BE
   REQUIRED?

2. *WHICH ARE THE MAIN*
   SEASONS OF INTEREST
   DESIRED?

3. *WHAT HEIGHT WILL BE PRACTICAL?*

4. *WHAT WIDTH WILL BE MOST USEFUL?*

5. *WILL EXTRA WIND TOLERANCE BE NEEDED?*

the crossword puzzle

Narrowing down these possibilities will be like doing a crossword puzzle. You start with a long description and work toward finding a single word. Here, the "description" will be the five key requirements. The "single word" will be the name of the plant (or plants) which fits that description. Frequently there will be more than one . . . but the trip to the nursery and seeing the plants available will make the final decision easy.
As mentioned earlier, that trip to the nursery where you can select the *specific* plant you like best (as well as terrace furnishings, etc.) is really the final step in planning the garden. Don't be afraid to experiment and don't be discouraged by a negative attitude on the part of salespeople in some garden centers. They really are a well-meaning lot, if too often pessimistic about any life on terraces or rooftops, especially in the city.

using the lists

The first two of the three lists which follow describe some generally reliable and widely available woody plants for use in terrace gardens. They are listed alphabetically by common name with the botanical one in parentheses below.
First, find the "light tolerance" column which applies to your conditions. Run your finger down that column and when you reach a plant which fits, check next to see if it is also suitable for your seasonal requirements. Then see if it sounds

appealing in any other way. Special note is made where narrow growing or espalier trainable plants exist within the genus listed.

The final column (pH range) is of little concern at this time. It refers to certain soil preferences which are discussed later on. For now, use it only to check general soil compatibility if you expect to have several woody plants in the same container.

The third list consists of plants which are normally grown outside only during the warm weather. Also listed alphabetically, the botanical names are omitted in most cases since they are in less frequent use.

Remember, your final decision will be made out at the nursery and, once there, don't be afraid to experiment and try plants you've never heard of before. Lists such as I've made here could not possibly be all inclusive. Therefore, think of them as a BEGINNING and not an end.

maneuvering
the budget

One final word: quality plant material frequently is expensive. This condition is aggravated greatly when one is beginning, since most terrace gardeners must buy both the soil ingredients and the container in which to plant. So take it easy and be patient. (The first rule for good gardeners anyway.) Everything does not have to be in place the first day of spring or even the first year of occupancy. Don't be afraid to let your plans grow and change just as the plants themselves will, over a period of time.

NAMES OF USEFUL TREES AND SHRUBS

PLANT NAMES & COMMENTS	ACCEPTABLE LIGHT CONDITIONS			
NOTE: **NV** = NARROW VARIETIES of this plant are available **FE** = FLAT or ESPALIER training possible	**FULL SUN**	**STRONG SUN** (midday or total up to 5 hours)	**WEAK SUN** (early or late day or total up to 3 hours)	**NO SUN** (some reflected light only)
AILANTHUS tree (Ailanthus) *Also called the "Tree of Heaven" this plant is to be used ONLY where all else has failed. A rapid grower which grows anywhere . . . it will also take over . . . anywhere. Avoid the males which have an offensive odor. It is easily transplanted, and some people consider this tree strictly "a weed".*	†	†	†	†
NV *ARBORVITAE tree or shrub sizes* (Thuja occidentalis) *This is a useful, versatile plant with many varieties available.*	†	†	†	†
AZALEA shrub (Azalea) *This is an excellent terrace plant; many flower colors are available. Buy only from nurseries as florists' plants are not usually hardy for cold winters outside.*	†	†	†	
BARBERRY shrub (Berberis) *Many varieties and leaf types are to be found, some trainable as hedges. Most are extremely wind-tolerant; a very useful group.*	†	†	†	†
NV *BIRCH tree* (Betula) *A graceful tree; weeping forms are also available. Its slow growth makes it useful for terraces.*	†	†	†	

SPECIAL SEASONAL INTEREST				pH RANGE
SPRING	SUMMER	FALL	WINTER	
Flowers		Leaf color		very tolerant
			Needle Evergreen	neutral to acid
Flowers		Leaf color	Broadleaf Evergreen (some deciduous)	acid
Flowers		Berries and leaf color	Some Broadleaf Evergreens	neutral to acid
Catkins		Leaf color	White bark and dried catkins	neutral to acid

PLANT NAMES & COMMENTS	FULL SUN	STRONG SUN	WEAK SUN	NO SUN
BLUEBERRY shrub (Vaccinum) These are excellent terrace plants; if treated properly they will bear pints of edible fruit. Two plants are needed for pollination.	†	†	†	
FE BUSH HONEYSUCKLE shrub (Lonicera tatarica) A tough little plant, this is trainable as a hedge or whatever you wish. May be planted bare root.	†	†	†	†
NV CALLERY PEAR tree (Pyrus calleryana) A good terrace plant; this hardy ornamental tree is now being used on some New York City streets.	†	†	†	
CHOKEBERRY shrub (Aronia brilliantissima) Different berry and leaf colors are available within this useful plant genus.	†	†	†	† (red variety)
FE COTONEASTER shrub (Cotoneaster) An extremely useful plant, of which many species are to be found; some are low and spreading, others trainable as uprights.	†	†	†	
FE NV CRAB APPLE tree (Malus) A good terrace plant with several flower colors, the fruit is useful for jelly only.	†	†	†	
FE DEUTZIA shrub (Deutzia) This is a rapid grower which often requires pruning to stay beautiful.	†	†	†	
DOGWOOD shrub or tree sizes (Cornus) There are many varieties to choose from, some of which do not like strong wind. In sunny areas, keep well watered.	†	†	†	† (few flowers)

SPRING	SUMMER	FALL	WINTER	pH RANGE
Flowers	Berries (time varies)	Leaf color	Branch form and color	very acid
Flowers	Berries	Leaf color		neutral to acid
Flowers		Leaf color		tolerant
Flowers	Berries	Leaf color		tolerant
Flowers		Berries Leaf color	Semi-Evergreen (in mild winters)	neutral to acid
Flowers	Fruit			neutral to acid
Flowers				neutral to acid
Flowers		Berries Leaf color		acid

NAMES OF USEFUL TREES AND SHRUBS (continued)

PLANT NAMES & COMMENTS	FULL SUN	STRONG SUN	WEAK SUN	NO SUN
NV FE *EUONYMUS shrub* (Euonymus) *Some are known as Burning Bush (because of fall color) or Spindle Tree (because of corky growths on branches). There are dozens of different species with varying leaf tones available. Typically common ones are* E. alatus *and* E. fortunei.	†	†	†	† *(some varieties)*
FE *FIRETHORN shrub* (Pyracantha coccinea) *A marvelous terrace plant with jagged unusual growth habit. Most varieties have long thorns.*	†	†	† *(few flowers)*	
FE NV *FLOWERING ALMOND shrub or tree sizes* (Prunus amygdalus) *No almonds, just beautiful flowers on a nice little plant.*	†	†	†	
NV FE *FLOWERING CHERRY shrub or tree sizes* (Prunus serrulata) *If you see a spring display (in the Brooklyn Botanic Garden for example) you will be impatient to have at least one for your terrace. Weeping forms and many flower colors available. Fruit of these types are generally inedible.*	†	†	†	
NV *FLOWERING QUINCE tree or shrub sizes* (Chaenomeles japonica) *A spectacular, though short, flowering time; the fruit may be used for jelly. This ornamental plant is sometimes sold as Cydonia.*	†	†	†	
FE *FORSYTHIA shrub* (Forsythia) *A brilliant way to welcome spring; strong pruning is required to keep this plant under control. Bare root planting is acceptable. Upright and weeping forms are available.*	†	†	† *(may flower poorly)*	

SPRING	SUMMER	FALL	WINTER	pH RANGE
Flowers		Berries Leaf color	Some Evergreen and Semi- Evergreen	neutral to acid
Flowers		Berries Leaf color	Semi- Evergreen (in mild winters)	neutral to acid
Flowers				neutral to acid
Flowers		(Flowering variety)		neutral to acid
Flowers				neutral to acid
Flowers				neutral to acid

NAMES OF USEFUL TREES AND SHRUBS (continued)

PLANT NAMES & COMMENTS	FULL SUN	STRONG SUN	WEAK SUN	NO SUN
NV *GINKGO tree* (Ginkgo) *Also known as Maidenhair Tree, this is a relic from prehistoric times. It is very hardy but slow-growing, so select one which is already interesting in form. The tree has fan-shaped leaves and the mature females bear pungent-smelling fruit prized as a delicacy by the Chinese.*	†	†	†	†
GOLD DUST PLANT shrub (Aucuba japonica) *Mottled, tropical-looking foliage covers this plant which likes moisture and protection from strong winds. Male and female flowers needed (separate plants) for berries.*		†	†	†
GOLDEN RAIN tree (Koelreuteria paniculata) *Unusual flowers and bark, this tree needs shelter from strong winds. New growth is reddish.*	†	†		
NV *HAWTHORN tree* (Crataegus) *Look for the newer disease and pest-resistant varieties; a wide range of shapes and sizes are available.*	†	†	†	
NV *HOLLY shrub or tree sizes* (Ilex) *Hundreds of different species are available, nearly all excellent for terrace use. Male and female plants often required for pollination. Most widely used are Japanese Holly, Inkberry, and American Holly. Select the leaf form you like the best.*	†	†	†	† *(some varieties)*
HONEY LOCUST tree (Gleditsia triacanthos) *Delicate-looking leaves on a very hardy tree; hanging seed pods are especially interesting.*	†	†	†	† *(some varieties)*
HYDRANGEA shrub (Hydrangea) *Useful for many terrace areas, some varieties may die back during severe winters.*	†	†	†	† *(some varieties)*

SPRING	SUMMER	FALL	WINTER	pH RANGE
		Leaf color		very tolerant
Flowers		Berries	Broadleaf Evergreen	neutral to acid
	Flowers	Berries		tolerant
Flowers		Berries Leaf color		neutral to acid
		Berries	Broadleaf Evergreen	acid
		Seed pods		neutral to acid
	Summer			acid = blue flowers alkaline = pink flowers

PLANT NAMES & COMMENTS	FULL SUN	STRONG SUN	WEAK SUN	NO SUN
JAPANESE MAPLE tree or shrub sizes (Acer palmatum) *Numerous leaf shapes and colors available as well as unusual dwarf varieties. Shelter from strong winds.*		†	†	† *(some varieties)*
NV FE *JUNIPER tree or shrub sizes* (Juniperus) *Dozens of different color tones and shapes available, making this a very versatile plant. Favorite varieties are the upright, pyramidal form* J. chinensis pyramidalis *and low-growing* J. horizontalis "Bar Harbor."	†	†	†	
LEUCOTHOE shrub (Leucothoe) *This is a graceful, low-growing addition for evergreen planting areas.*		†	†	†
LINDEN tree (Tilia cordata) *The silver-leaf varieties of this tree add interest and contrast to the garden.*	†	†	†	
MAGNOLIA tree or shrub sizes (Magnolia) *This is a beautiful plant when properly pruned; choose locally hardy varieties.*	†	†	† *(few flowers)*	
FE *MOCK ORANGE shrub* (Philadelphus) *Very sweet flowers on a bushy-growing shrub; good pruning will keep it under control.*	†	†	†	† *(few flowers)*
MOUNTAIN ASH tree (Sorbus americana) *Several varieties exist of this delicate-looking but very hardy tree. A slow growth habit makes it good for terrace use.*	†	†	†	
OREGON GRAPE shrub (Mahonia aquifolium) *Useful for poor light conditions, this plant prefers wind-protected spots.*		†	†	†

SPRING	SUMMER	FALL	WINTER	pH RANGE
(leaf colors sometimes vary throughout)				*tolerant*
		Berries (some varieties)	*Needle Evergreen*	*neutral*
Flowers		*Leaf color*	*Broadleaf Evergreen*	*very acid*
	Flowers			*neutral to acid*
Flowers				*neutral to acid*
	Flowers			*neutral to acid*
Flowers		*Berries Leaf color*		*acid*
	Flowers	*Berries Leaf color*	*Broadleaf Evergreen*	*tolerant*

NAMES OF USEFUL TREES AND SHRUBS (continued)

PLANT NAMES & COMMENTS	FULL SUN	STRONG SUN	WEAK SUN	NO SUN
PEA TREE tree (Caragana) *Also known as Siberian Pea, this small, very hardy tree has delicate-looking leaves. Weeping forms are available. Withstands strong winds.*	†	†	†	
PEPPERBUSH shrub (Clethra alnifolia) *Also known as Summersweet, this plant does not like dry conditions.*	†	†	†	† *(few flowers)*
NV *PIERIS JAPONICA shrub* (Pieris japonica) *Also known as Lily of the Valley shrub or Andromeda, this excellent terrace plant has reddish new growth.*	†	†	†	†
NV FE *PINE tree or shrub sizes* (Pinus) *Dozens of useful shapes and colors available for many terrace needs. Especially useful for windy areas is Japanese Black Pine* (P. thunbergii), *a bushy low-growing variety is the Dwarf Mugho Pine* (P. mugo mughus).	†	†	†	†
NV FE *PRIVET tree or shrub sizes* (Ligustrum) *Exceptionally useful for many purposes, these plants grow under difficult conditions and withstand high winds. Bare root planting acceptable.*	†	†	†	†
PURPLE LEAF PLUM tree or shrub sizes (Prunus cerasifera pissardii) *A graceful plant with lovely contrasting foliage color; look for newer disease-resistant varieties.*	†	†	† *(color may fade)*	
NV FE *PUSSY WILLOW shrub or tree sizes* (Salix discolor) *This is a rapid grower which needs lots of water; bare root planting acceptable.*	†	†	†	†

SPRING	SUMMER	FALL	WINTER	pH RANGE
Flowers				neutral to acid
	Flowers	Leaf color		acid
Flowers			Broadleaf Evergreen	very acid
	Cones		Needle Evergreen	neutral to acid
	Flowers	Berries	Semi-Evergreen (in mild winters)	
Flowers				neutral
Catkins				neutral to acid

NAMES OF USEFUL TREES AND SHRUBS (continued)

PLANT NAMES & COMMENTS	FULL SUN	STRONG SUN	WEAK SUN	NO SUN
REDBUD shrub or tree sizes (Cercis canadensis) *Also known as Judas Tree, it prefers a wind-sheltered spot.*	†	†	†	
RHODODENDRON shrub (Rhododendron) *Many flower colors and leaf shapes are available. Some leaf burning occurs in very exposed, dry areas; otherwise a good addition.*		†	†	† *(few flowers)*
FE *ROSE MALLOW shrub* (Hibiscus) *There are hundreds of species of this flowering plant one of which is known as Rose of Sharon. Buy only locally hardy specimens and keep well pruned for a good appearance. Most of the typically large flowers are bell-shaped.*	†	†	†	† *(few flowers)*
NV *ROSE shrub* (Rosa) *This is an excellent terrace plant, not at all difficult for beginners. Buy only from reputable dealers and keep plants well-fertilized. Floribundas are best to start with. Bare root planting is acceptable, but pre-potted types are easier. Several useful varieties are "Gene Boerner", "Spartan", "Jiminy Cricket", and "Woburn Abbey".*	†	†	† *(some varieties)*	
RUSSIAN OLIVE shrub or tree sizes (Elaeagnus angustifolia) *A very hardy plant which withstands high winds, its beautiful silvery foliage may also be trimmed as a hedge.*	†	†	†	†
SHADBLOW shrub or tree sizes (Amelanchier canadensis) *Also known as Service-Berry or Shadbush; this plant withstands moderately windy conditions.*	†	†	†	† *(few flowers)*
SKIMMIA shrub (Skimmia) *Use only locally hardy varieties; male and female plants required for berries.*	†	†	†	

SPRING	SUMMER	FALL	WINTER	pH RANGE
Flowers		*Leaf color*		*neutral*
Flowers			*Broadleaf Evergreen*	*very acid*
	Flowers			*neutral to acid*
	Flowers			*neutral to acid*
	Flowers			*neutral to alkaline*
Flowers	*Berries*	*Leaf color*		*neutral to acid*
Flowers		*Berries*	*Broadleaf Evergreen*	*neutral to acid*

NAMES OF USEFUL TREES AND SHRUBS (continued)

PLANT NAMES & COMMENTS	FULL SUN	STRONG SUN	WEAK SUN	NO SUN
SOURWOOD tree (Oxydendrum arboreum) *Also known as Sorreltree or Lily of the Valley tree; its slow growth makes it a useful addition. Does not like extreme winds; otherwise highly recommended.*	†	†	†	† *(few flowers)*
FE *SPIREA shrub* (Spiraea) *Also known as Bridal Wreath; this rapidly growing shrub requires good pruning to keep it shapely.*	†	†	†	† *(few flowers)*
NV *SPRUCE tree or shrub sizes* (Picea) *Numerous useful shapes and color tones of spruces are available.*	†	†	†	
SWEET SHRUB shrub (Calycanthus floridus) *Also known as Carolina Allspice; the flowers have a spicy scent. The glossy foliage adds contrast.*	†	†	†	† *(few flowers)*
NV FE *TAMARISK shrub or tree sizes* (Tamarix pentandra) *Unusual flower form and silvery leaves; pruning is required to keep this plant from taking over. Tolerant of extreme winds.*	†	†	†	
NV *VIBURNUM shrub and tree sizes* (Viburnum) *Hundreds of species for every taste and location. Take your pick!*	†	†	†	† *(some varieties)*

SPRING	SUMMER	FALL	WINTER	pH RANGE
	Flowers	Seed pods Leaf color		acid
	Flowers			neutral to acid
			Needle Evergreen	acid
Flowers				neutral
	Flowers			
Flowering, (time varies with variety)		Berries	Semi- Evergreen (varieties)	neutral to acid

NAMES OF USEFUL TREES AND SHRUBS (continued)

PLANT NAMES & COMMENTS	FULL SUN	STRONG SUN	WEAK SUN	NO SUN
WEEPING WILLOW tree (Salix) *If you're a masochist who loves beautiful things, this is the tree for you. QUANTITIES of water are required for its rapid growing root system . . . or it drops its leaves and dies back immediately. Must be root-pruned severely periodically (not easy with these tough roots). A difficult terrace plant, but true willow-lovers are equally so. Not recommended (don't say I didn't warn you).*	†	†	†	†
WEIGELA tree or shrub sizes (Weigela) *Severe winters may cause die-back in exposed conditions. A good grower requiring pruning to keep in shape.*	†	†	†	† *(few flowers)*
WITCH HAZEL tree or shrub sizes (Hamamelis) *The cold-weather flowering period makes this plant useful for terraces.*	†	†	†	† *(few flowers)*
NV *YEW shrub* (Taxus) *Various shapes and needle tones are available making this plant useful for many situations. Widely used are the Japanese Upright* (T. cuspidata capitata), *shrubby spreading "Hatfield"* (Taxus media hatfieldii) *and a nearly upright "Hicks"* (T. media Hicksii).	†	†	†	† *(some varieties)*

SPRING	SUMMER	FALL	WINTER	pH RANGE
Catkins			Branch color and form	tolerant
	Flowers			neutral
		Flowers . . . (time varies with variety)		acid
		Berries	Needle Evergreen	neutral

NAMES OF USEFUL WOODY VINES AND CLIMBERS

PLANT NAMES & COMMENTS	ACCEPTABLE LIGHT CONDITIONS			
	FULL SUN	STRONG SUN (midday or total up to 5 hours)	WEAK SUN (early or late day or total up to 3 hours)	NO SUN (some reflected light only)
BITTERSWEET (Celastrus) *Colorful fall fruit adorns these rapid growers; male and female plants are required to insure pollination.*	†	†	†	
CLEMATIS (Clematis) *This plant has large showy flowers freely produced in a variety of colors. It is also known as Virgin's Bower.*	†	†	†	
CLIMBING HYDRANGEA (Hydrangea) *The lovely, delicate white blooms of this plant in no way resemble those of the typical hydrangea shrub. This plant will cling by itself to masonry if the wind is not too strong. Plant does not bloom until well established and mature, but is a nice addition anyway.*	†	†	†	
CLIMBER ROSES *For nearly continual summer bloom roses are my favorite and those which climb are especially useful. Buy locally hardy varieties. Several good bloomers are "Blaze", "Golden Showers", and "Don Juan". "Golden Showers" has very few thorns, which makes it all the more desirable.*	†	†	† (some varieties)	

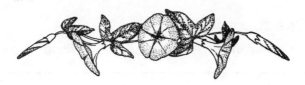

SPECIAL SEASONAL INTEREST				pH RANGE
SPRING	SUMMER	FALL	WINTER	
		Berries (last through winter)		very tolerant
	Flowers (time varies with variety)			alkaline
	Flowers (early summer)			neutral to acid
	Flowers			neutral to acid

WOODY VINES & CLIMBERS (continued)

PLANT NAMES & COMMENTS	FULL SUN	STRONG SUN	WEAK SUN	NO SUN
EUONYMUS (Euonymus) *Also known by other names, including Wintercreeper, there are many useful climbers in this genus. Of especial interest are two of the evergreen species,* E. fortunei *and* E. patens. *Many varieties are susceptible to scale insects.*	†	†	†	† *(some varieties)*
HONEYSUCKLE (Lonicera) *A twining vine which needs something to hold on to, it will quickly take over a problem area. Keep it off your trees! Yellow or pinkish purple flowers are typical and some are extremely fragrant. The strong roots may choke off weaker plants in the same container.*	†	†	†	† *(may flower poorly)*
IVY *Many ivies are available, either for use as trailers or for covering walls. Buy only locally hardy varieties for outdoor use. Two of the most common are English Ivy* (Hedera helix) *and Boston Ivy* (Parthenocissus tricuspidata). *One especially hardy ivy in the New York City area is the English variety "238th Street", developed by The New York Botanical Garden.*	†	†	†	†
SILVERLACE (Polygonum aubertii) *Sometimes known as China Fleece or Silver Fleece; the fluffy white flowers produced in profusion give a cloud-like appearance. A very rapid grower once established, this vine will quickly take over a problem fence.*	†	†	†	†
VIRGINIA CREEPER (Parthenocissus quinquefolia) *This energetic climber will grab on to nearly anything and quickly cover a problem wall. Keep it OFF your trees.*	†	†	†	†

SPRING	SUMMER	FALL	WINTER	pH RANGE
Flowers		Berries	Evergreen and Semi-Evergreen varieties	very tolerant
	Flowers			very tolerant
		Leaf color (Boston Ivy)	Evergreen species (English Ivy)	neutral to acid
	Flowers (late summer)			very tolerant
		Leaf color		very tolerant

NAMES OF USEFUL WARM WEATHER FLOWERS & OTHER SMALL PLANTS

PLANT NAMES & COMMENTS

ACCEPTABLE LIGHT CONDITIONS

PLANT NAMES & COMMENTS	FULL SUN	STRONG SUN (midday or total under 5 hours)	WEAK SUN (early or late day or total up to 3 hours)	NO SUN (some reflected light only)
AGERATUM (annual) *This plant has fluffy-looking blue, purple, or pink flowers, and likes rich soil and water. Pinching off dead blooms promotes additional flowering.*	†	†		
AJUGA (perennial) *Also known as Bugleweed; this plant does well under poor growing conditions. It has early summer flowers and fall leaf color; leaves form a dense, mat-like cover.*	†	†	†	†
ALYSSUM (perennials and annuals) *This plant has a carpet-like cover of small flowers usually white or purple. Remove spent flowers for additional bloom.*	†	†		
ASTER (perennials and annuals) *Available in many different colors; keep spent flowers cut to promote additional bloom. Some varieties are very disease-prone.*	†	†		
BALLOON FLOWER (perennial) (Platycodon grandiflorum) *A graceful ground cover which gets straggly if left unchecked for several years; the mid-summer purple flowers are cup-shaped.*	†	†		
BALSAM (annual) *Small, neat bunches which grow best in rich, moist soil; the flower colors are pinks, reds, and purples.*	†	†		
BASIL (annual) *This is an attractive herb, easily grown from seed and useful for salads. The ornamental variety with burgundy leaves is a nice addition to the summer garden. The flowers are white or lavender but should be pinched off to promote leaf growth for kitchen use.*	†	†	†	

74

PLANT NAMES & COMMENTS	FULL SUN	STRONG SUN	WEAK SUN	NO SUN
BEGONIA (perennial) Many varieties of this excellent plant are available for terrace use. Flowers are usually white, red, or pinkish. Interesting leaf shapes and colors available; many useful for hanging baskets. Not hardy in cold areas, all may be taken indoors for the winter. A good versatile plant.	†	†	†	† (may not flower)
BLACK-EYED SUSAN VINE (annual) Sometimes called a Clock Vine; the yellow flowers make a cheerful-looking plant useful for hanging baskets as well as a fence covering.	†	†	†	
CALADIUM (perennial) Large, delicate-looking foliage adds a beautiful contrast in sheltered spots. The green or red leaves are streaked with white and produce an unusual flower. The tuberous root is not hardy in cold areas and may be taken indoors for planting the following year.		†	†	†
CARDINAL CLIMBER VINE (annual) A rapid grower, easily grown from seed; if provided with string for support it will quickly cover any area. Trumpet-shaped flowers are red, foliage delicate-looking.	†	†		
CELOSIA (annual) Also known as Cockscomb, which is a good description of one of the two varieties of flowers. The other resembles a feathery plume. A good terrace plant; the long-lasting red, orange, or yellow flowers may be dried and preserved.	†	†	†	
CHIVES (perennial) A useful kitchen herb which has grass-like, long (round) leaves and grows in bunches. If left uncut, little red-purplish flowers appear. It's best to buy pots of plants rather than attempt to grow from seed.	†	†	†	

WARM WEATHER FLOWERS & OTHER SMALL PLANTS (continued)

PLANT NAMES & COMMENTS	FULL SUN	STRONG SUN	WEAK SUN	NO SUN
CHRYSANTHEMUM (perennial) *The hothouse plants from florists rarely make it through a cold winter outside, but they are useful additions for as long as they live. A good range of yellow and orange varieties available, with many flower shapes to choose from. For continuous bloom, keep well watered and remove spent flowers.*	†	†	†	
CLEOME (annual) *Also known as Spider Flower, this is an excellent terrace plant, easily grown from seed. Pinch the growing tip to keep it shorter and force side shoots for flowering. The pink- or white-colored flowers gain in intensity as the sun sets.*	†	†	†	
COLEUS (perennial) *Also known as Painted Nettle, this plant may be taken in for the winter in cold areas. Most people prefer to grow it for its variegated red, purple, white, and green foliage. It also provides a spiky flower.*	†	†	†	† *(colors will fade)*
CORN (annual) *Believe it or not, corn is a good terrace plant and is easily grown from seed. Be sure to get the eating, "sweet corn" varieties. Grow a minimum of 3 plants, if possible, to insure pollination.*	†	†		
COSMOS (annual) *Delicate-looking foliage is produced on this tough plant which is easily grown from seed. Many different bright colors of freely produced flowers appear on each plant.*	†	†	†	
CROCUS (perennial) *A beautiful way to fill the gap between the gray of winter and the glory of spring: plant lots of crocus in late fall. They may be dug up after the leaves have died and stored for replanting yearly. Colors are usually a cheerful assortment of yellows, purples, and whites.*	†	†	†	†

PLANT NAMES & COMMENTS	FULL SUN	STRONG SUN	WEAK SUN	NO SUN
CROTON (perennial) *The colorful, long, sword-like leaves of this tropical plant are useful for brightening dark spots in the garden. Plant may be taken indoors for the cold winter.*		†	†	†
CUCUMBER (perennial) *Very rich soil, hot days, and lots of water will yield a good cucumber crop. Keep removing the fruit to insure production of more.*	†	†		
CYPRESS VINE (annual) *A rapid grower with very fine, fern-like leaves, this plant with red or white flowers is easily grown from seed.*	†	†		
DAFFODIL (perennial) *A nice plant if you've room to spare, daffodils multiply quickly when left in the soil from year to year. The yellow or white trumpet shaped flowers welcome the spring.*	†	†	†	†
DAHLIA (perennial) *Many colorful flower types available; most varieties prefer rich soil and plenty of moisture. The tubers may be stored for replanting yearly.*	†	†		
DAY LILY (perennial) *The botanical name (Hemerocallis) means "beautiful for one day," and that's a perfect description. Sword-shaped leaves and a wide variety of colored flowers. Don't attempt them if you're short on container space.*	†	†	†	† *(some varieties)*
DILL (annual) *Both the fruit and leaves of this feathery plant are useful in the kitchen. The unusual ball-shaped flowers are yellow.*	†	†		
DUSTY MILLER (perennial) *Beautiful silvery-gray leaves on this plant will add contrast to any summer garden. The small yellow flowers are of less interest than the foliage. It will survive mild winters.*	†	†	†	

WARM WEATHER FLOWERS & OTHER SMALL PLANTS (continued)

PLANT NAMES & COMMENTS	FULL SUN	STRONG SUN	WEAK SUN	NO SUN
FERNS *(perennial)* *Hundreds of species of ferns are available for the summer garden as well as all year long. Some may be tropical in origin and must be taken in during cold winters but others are hardy for year-round outdoor use. There are many leaf shapes and color tones to choose from. Most fern species prefer the rich, moist soils, often found in deep forest conditions. Thus, these are exceptionally useful plants for poor light spots.*		†	†	†
FOUR O'CLOCK *This plant produces freely blooming flowers which open in late afternoon. Easily grown from seed; there are many flower colors.*	†	†		
FUCHSIA *(perennial)* *A cool, wind-sheltered spot is best for these beautiful flowers. Often used in hanging baskets, which may be taken indoors for the winter. The flowers are in pinks or shades of purple with white. (Watch out for white flies.)*		†	†	
GERANIUM *(perennial)* *If there is a "classic" summer flower it is probably the geranium. In cold areas they may be taken in and kept as houseplants, often blooming throughout the winter (although they are given a quiet "rest period" by some). The bushy flowers come in reds, pinks, and whites and a variety of leaf shapes and growing habits. Kept well fed, they will bloom all summer.*	†	†	† *(fewer flowers)*	
HENS & CHICKENS *(perennial)* *Also known as House Leeks or Live-Forevers (translated from the botanical Sempervivum), these tough little plants are very useful for dry, poor soil areas. They are mostly green with edges of reddish shades; leaf shapes vary. Some survive mild winter conditions outside.*	†	†	†	
HOUSEPLANTS *Any and all houseplants may spend the summer outside. Introduce them gradually to stronger sun and wind conditions.*	†	†	†	†

(same as inside)

PLANT NAMES & COMMENTS	FULL SUN	STRONG SUN	WEAK SUN	NO SUN
IMPATIENS (annual) This is an excellent terrace plant for nearly every condition. Several varieties are available, including one with reddish leaves. The red, pink, or white flowers are freely borne all summer through to the first killing frost.	†	†	†	†
LANTANA (perennial) Useful for the summer garden, this plant with its many colored flowers survives poor soil and difficult growing conditions. Pinching off the spent flowers promotes bloom. (If you take it indoors in cold-weather areas, watch out for white flies.)	†	†	†	
LILY OF THE VALLEY (perennial) The delicate-looking white flowers which appear in the spring make this a useful plant for shade conditions. Hardy in cold winters, the plants multiply slowly, eventually forming a dense mat.		†	†	†
LOBELIA (annuals and perennials) Easily grown from seed; the hanging varieties are especially useful. The annual flowered ones are blue, the perennials are red. If they get too straggly, pinch back.		†	†	† (may not flower well)
LUPINE (annuals and perennials) A well-watered, cool spot is best for this plant which is useful for poor light conditions. The flower colors are many and resemble "fairy wings," the translation of its botanical name.		†	†	†
MARIGOLD (annual) A cheerful addition to any garden; remove the spent flowers to promote bloom. Keep undersides well washed to prevent buildup of mites. The flowers are in an assortment of yellows and oranges.	†	†	† (few flowers)	
MARJORAM (annual) A graceful plant with purple-pink flowers, the leaves may be used as seasoning for poultry, salads, and decoration on food. The leaves may also be dried and stored for future use in the kitchen.	†	†		

WARM WEATHER FLOWERS & OTHER SMALL PLANTS (continued)

PLANT NAMES & COMMENTS	FULL SUN	STRONG SUN	WEAK SUN	NO SUN
MINT *(perennial)* *Several mints useful as kitchen herbs as well as decorative summer plants are spearmint, peppermint, and applemint. All are scented and produce spires of flowers in purples, pinks, or white. Roots may survive cold weather if well covered.*		†	†	†
MOONFLOWER VINE *(annual)* *A useful vine because of its late-afternoon flowering habit; the white blooms open as the day fades. This plant is easily started from seed and is a good grower.*	†	†	†	
MORNING GLORY *(annual)* *Easily grown from seed, this plant prefers poor soil. A delightful way to start the day is to watch the pink, blue, or purple flowers open. Keep foliage well hosed to prevent buildup of insects.*	†	†	† *(few flowers)*	
NASTURTIUMS *(annual)* *These plants do not like rich soil and will produce only lush foliage with no flowers if grown in it. Useful for hanging baskets and easily grown from seed; the leaves are prized for salads and the flowers for food decoration. If buildup of insects occurs keep foliage well hosed.*	†	†	†	
PACHYSANDRA *(perennial)* *A tough, evergreen, this plant is often used as a ground cover where all else has failed. Some varieties produce spiky-looking spring flowers.*	†	†	†	†
PANSY *(biennial)* *Cheerful little faces in an assortment of yellows or purples make the pansy a favorite of many. To promote new blooms, remove all spent flowers.*	†	†	† *(fewer flowers)*	

PLANT NAMES & COMMENTS	FULL SUN	STRONG SUN	WEAK SUN	NO SUN
PARSLEY (biennial) *Useful for food decoration as well as an excellent source of vitamins, parsley is easy to grow and cut fresh as needed. The curly leaf is favored by many, but the flat one is my favorite. Parsley likes rich soil and continues to grow well into the cold weather. It sets seed and does poorly the second year; better to start again.*		†	†	
PERIWINKLE (annual) *An excellent flowering plant for many difficult spots, this annual form of Vinca, with its red, pink, or white blooms, is highly recommended.*	†	†	†	† (fewer flowers)
PETUNIA (annual) *Another classic summer flower, these plants favor rich soil and generous waterings. Remove spent flowers to promote continual bloom and cut back severely if they become too leggy. Useful for hanging baskets. May become insect-infested towards the end of the summer. If so, cut back severely or discard.*	†	†	† (fewer flowers)	
PHLOX (annuals and perennials) *A light soil is preferred by these plants which have bunches of small flowers in shades of red, pink, and white. Dead flowers must be removed to promote added blooms.*	†	†		
PRIMROSE (annuals and perennials) *A compact plant with neat, colorful flowers in many shades, the roots may survive mild winters.*		†	†	†
PORTULACA (annual) *This is one of the toughest, most useful little summer flowers. Absolutely recommended for sunny locations, it will survive hot, exposed spots, all the while producing a profusion of color rivaled by few others. The flowers close as the sun disappears. Apparently untouched by disease or pests, it will self-sow easily wherever it can.*	†	†		

WARM WEATHER FLOWERS & OTHER SMALL PLANTS (continued)

PLANT NAMES & COMMENTS	FULL SUN	STRONG SUN	WEAK SUN	NO SUN
RUDBECKIA *(perennial)* *This is another tough, virtually indestructible, colorful flower. Also known as Gloriosa Daisy, this plant is good for exposed locations. The large yellow flowers bloom all summer.*	†	†	† *(fewer flowers)*	
SALPIGLOSSIS *(annual)* *Easily grown from seed, this flower comes in a wide range of colors. It is also useful for hanging baskets.*	†	†	†	
SALVIA *(perennial)* *A good addition to the summer garden; the red or blue flowers are shaped like small spikes and are rather long-lasting.*	†	†	†	
SEDUM *(perennial)* *A tough little plant, also known as Creeping Charlie or Stonecrop, it will survive in the poorest of soils or growing conditions. The most widely available variety has small yellow, early spring flowers. Survives long periods with little water.*	†	†	†	†
SNAPDRAGON *(annuals and perennials)* *Unusual long-spiked flowers in an assortment of color choices make this a favorite in many gardens. Some are very disease- or pest-prone. The removal of spent flowers is essential for additional bloom.*	†	†	† *(few flowers)*	
SPIDERWORT *(perennial)* *Also known by its botanical name Tradescantia, this plant is sometimes called Wandering Jew. The showy, purplish leaves are long and narrow, useful for hanging baskets. Small flowers appear if the plant is kept well fertilized. In cold-weather areas, it may be taken indoors and kept as a houseplant.*	†	†	†	
SUNFLOWER *(annual)* *Exceptionally easy to grow from seed, these plants should not be expected to share their container with anything else. A delightful flower if you've room to spare, it will thrive in any soil, so long as the sunlight is strong and the watering generous.*	†	†		

PLANT NAMES & COMMENTS	FULL SUN	STRONG SUN	WEAK SUN	NO SUN
THYME *(perennial)* This is a dainty plant which will survive neglect. The leaves are grayish green and useful as a seasoning. It is easily grown from seed. The flower is a purplish color.	†	†	†	
TOMATO *(annual)* There is nothing so delicious as eating a freshly picked tomato, especially from your own garden. There are small "cherry tomato" plants as well as the full-size ones. The latter look neater when supported on a stake at least 4 feet in height, although some gardeners allow the plants to flop about on the ground. Keep well watered, especially on very hot days. Extreme hot drying winds may cause the blossoms to drop off.	†	†	† *(some varieties)*	
TULIP *(perennials)* By planting these bulbs in late fall you will assure yourself of a beautiful and colorful spring. Highly hybridized varieties rarely repeat their bloom, but others may be removed after their leaves have died and can be stored away for replanting yearly.	†	†	†	†
VERBENA *(perennial)* These colorful little plants may be taken indoors during the cold winter. They survive poor soil and dry conditions. (Watch out for white flies.)	†	†		
ZINNIA *(annual)* Brightly colored flowers will be borne in great profusion if the spent ones are removed promptly. The ability to tolerate heat and the wide range of flower colors make this a useful terrace plant.	†	†	† *(may not flower well)*	

A number of plants mentioned in this section, in common use in many gardens, are poisonous to varying degrees if eaten or chewed. I have taught my children to put *nothing* from the garden in their mouths, except those plant *parts* which I have specifically said are okay . . . such as the berries from the blueberry shrub only, and not just blue-colored berries, or the tomato fruit only, from the tomato plant, etc.

Rather than eliminate "dangerous" plants altogether (probably impossible to do anyway), I feel it's better to teach them now to have respect for potentially lethal members of the plant kingdom. I have made it clear what may happen if they choose otherwise . . . And as Dr. Peter K. Nelson of the Brooklyn Botanic Garden told me recently, humans should not assume a plant is safe to eat just because they see a cat, dog, or bird eating it. This is an unfortunate misconception.

The following is a list of some of the plants with *parts* (stems, leaves, etc.) known to have caused serious or fatal illness when eaten or chewed:

Azalea	Poinsettia
English Ivy	Oleander
Yew	Lily of the Valley
Foxglove	Holly
Iris	Crocus
Caladium	Narcissus
Lantana	Peach trees
Mountain Laurel	Cherry trees
Rhododendron	Daffodil
Larkspur	

Symptoms of plant poisoning vary considerably but may include pain, drowsiness, or vomiting. If you suspect it, don't attempt to treat it yourself! Instead, immediately call your Poison Control Center, as well as your doctor. Describe the plant you believe to be the cause and be sure to bring a portion with you if you go to a hospital.

Some of these plants are lovely though, so please don't let the thought of being harmed by them affect your gardening selections. A little respect for plants in general will always hold you in good stead.

Some terrace gardens explained

The following photographs reveal details of plant life on several terraces, thus revealing how these gardens were achieved.

HANGING GERANIUM

JAPANESE CHERRY TREE

CRAB-APPLE TREES

BIRCH TREE

FLORIBUNDA ROSE

CLIMBING ROSE

BEGONIA

PORTULACA

CLEOME

WEEPING WILLOW   PRIVETS   BLACK PINE

TULIPS   PIERIS JAPONICA   JUNIPER

87

WEEPING WILLOW

PIERIS JAPONICA

PRIVETS

MARIGOLDS

CLIMBING ROSES

ZINNIAS

MARIGOLDS

CLIMBING HYDRANGEA

CLIMBING EVERGREEN EUONYMUS

"P.G." HYDRANGEA   CRAB-APPLE TREE

ASPARAGUS FERN

AZALEA

PORTULACA

IMPATIENS

ZINNIAS

CLIMBING ROSE

89

SILVERLACE VINE

BOSTON IVY

PRIVET HEDGE

SPRUCE TREE

ENGLISH IVY

BLACK PINE TREE
(Mostly hidden in photograph)

COTONEASTER

SPRUCE TREE

BOSTON IVY   FUCHSIA   IMPATIENS

MOUNTAIN ASH TREE

LOBELIA

PETUNIAS

PORTULACA

DAHLIA

DUSTY MILLER

ALYSSUM

HELIOTROPE

BLUE SPRUCE

CRAB APPLE
(*Mostly hidden in photograph*)

RHODODENDRON

BEGONIA

DWARF ALBERTA SPRUCE

92

QUINCE TREE
(*Mostly hidden in photograph*)

PIERIS JAPONICA

VIRGINIA CREEPER

CRAB-APPLE TREE

GERANIUM

MARIGOLDS

RHODODENDRON

A long-forgotten thing;
     a pot where now a flower blooms—
          this day of spring!
                         Shiki

Section 4

Our Plants Live in Containers

People sometimes ask me if I "take in the trees for
the winter." I realize this question is not asked in
jest . . . but the idea of bringing a tall birch tree,
mountain ash, or two crab apples into an apartment
surely must be considered a joke.

our plants are
outside all year What they are really asking, however, is: "How is it
possible for container trees and shrubs to remain
outdoors (in New York City) *all winter long* and
live?"

It has been proved to me time and again that nearly
any plant which survives in the vicinity, outside, in
the ground, can also be grown outside, above the
ground, although it may take a bit more work.

Hardy trees and shrubs die during the winter
primarily from one of two causes. First, the rapid,
alternate freezing and thawing may tear or injure
too much of the root system. Soil is a natural
insulator, so plants growing in the Earth itself are
winter-kill of
roots sufficiently protected against all but unusually severe
frosts. The deeper their roots and the more soil
between them and the cold, the greater the
protection.

The other reason plants may falter in the winter is
because even in their dormant state they need
minute quantities of both nutrients and water.

Again, the more soil present, the greater the area in which food and moisture can be retained.

If we apartment dwellers wish to have a long-lived and healthy garden, we must strive to duplicate those root level conditions which sustain plant life in the ground. And helping us do this is the primary function of our plant's container. The more soil present the better off will be that root system, the plant, and, ultimately, the terrace owner. This is true not only during the winter but all year long.

the "ideal" container

Thus it appears that an ideal solution might be to have a large masonry planter stretching from one end of the terrace to the other. This would provide maximum soil area and would be extremely durable as well.

If you can afford it, in terms of both space and money, this is certainly the thing to do. And, if you do attempt this ideal solution, get the most reliable and experienced landscape contractor available for the planning and building. This is an extremely specialized area and no place for an ordinary bricklayer.

But "ideal solutions" are rarely attainable and if yours is a high-rise apartment this is no exception. Assuming you are able to locate a good contractor, you may find yourself limited by several other factors. Stringent building codes, for example, look unkindly on constructing permanent heavy additions onto an already completed structure. Masonry walls for such a planter are really a major building change and may drastically alter the existing conditions. Soil is not light and pushes sideways as well as downward, a potential hazard to parapet walls. In addition, you may be unable or unwilling to commit yourself to such an expenditure, especially if a short-rental lease is involved.

But more importantly, there is the real possibility, NEVER, NEVER TO BE FORGOTTEN, of leaks to the apartments below . . . not easy to repair if you've built something *permanent* and *immovable* on top of them! All of which leads to the conclusion that the apparently "ideal solution" is not always so "ideal" after all. And it is with this in mind that many terrace gardeners use the alternative "practical solution": separate containers for all the plants. As far as I'm concerned there are more than enough advantages in this method to sufficiently offset any disadvantages.

the practical
solution

Returning now to the discussion about winter survival, the need for a large container has been established. However, from the practical point of view our containers also have to be small enough for us to handle and deal with. This includes being able to fit through the window or door. The philosophy "a miss is as good as a mile" is unfortunately all too applicable here . . . since as little as a half inch too wide to fit can be a real disaster!

Thus it is useful to establish as a rule of thumb a *minimum* tub size which on one hand will sustain life outside all year long, yet still be practical for small terrace use. In New York City, where I live, I have found that this safe minimum diameter is about 14 inches (35 cm.). This minimum applies to *every* direction—height, length, width.

minimum size

In colder areas to the north, the minimum should be increased several inches, while to the south, it may be reduced.

But remember, wherever possible, depending on available space (and budget), *it is better to exceed this minimum size.*

Some nurserymen may consider 14 inches a rather conservative figure, which it well may be. For in fact, there is no single magic number exactly right for every plant or terrace condition. Extremely hardy plant varieties undoubtedly will survive the cold in smaller containers but the watering and feeding chores will rise proportionately the rest of the year and this must not be discounted from a practical point of view.

but bigger is
better

In any event, my conservative minimum has not failed me yet so I unhesitatingly recommend it as a point from which to begin.

If you are of the do-it-yourself school, here's where you certainly can. Although it's possible to build a planter of large stones, the most popular homemade material is wood. As it's important to have a *bottom* to your planter so that you can move it when you want to or have to, the most popular material turns out to be most practical as well. If possible, buy lumber of durable stock, such as redwood or cedar, specifying to the lumberman, who can cut it to size for you, that it be free of knots or other weaknesses. The wood should have a minimum thickness of ¾ inch, and more if you are planning a large planter. Rustproof screws are essential and angle irons or brackets useful; the container will be subject to alternate wetting and drying as well as the ravages of the weather. Redwood and cedar require no preservative but may cost more than you wish to spend.

some basics for
building with
wood

When we built our first planter, we used pine. Upon completion, it was a large, clumsy-looking thing which rather resembled a coffin but it did fit perfectly into one complete corner of our small balcony.

To assure our work's longevity, we stained all sides several times (thereby giving pine the elegance of walnut) and drilled several holes in the bottom for drainage. Then we completely covered the inside faces with a preservative to prevent decay. I believe we used tar paint, which is not toxic to plants. But now many other excellent preservatives may be found at hardware stores, which are not as messy and will also seal the wood's surface. One such product recommended by nursery supplier Al Saffer & Co. is Cuprinol® for Florists, Number 14. He ships everywhere so you can write to him at 130 West 28 Street, New York, N.Y. 10001 for his free catalogue of many useful products. Horticulturist Al Nordheden informs me additionally that the University of Illinois Agricultural College warns against the use of products having creosote or pentachlorophenol, as these are highly toxic to plants.

Our planter was deemed complete after we added several wood strips for "legs" to raise it off the floor, thereby reducing bottom rot. Over ten years later, although we had long since moved from that

apartment, both the planter and some of the original plants were still around and faring well . . . How much longer it will all last is anybody's guess, but it is apparent that with a little care a homemade planter can be quite satisfactory.

However, that was the first and last time we made our own. We soon discovered that it is often easier and well worth any additional expense to select a

container which already exists. And there is certainly a great deal to choose from.

ready-made
planters

Among the most widely available and practical ready-made containers are the simple boxes of redwood, held together by steel bands. Yet a mind-boggling assortment of shapes, sizes, and styles are available not only in wood but in asbestos-cement, fiberglass, and even ornate sculptured stone, cast cement, and terra cotta. (Terra cotta may crack under severe cold conditions.) Garden centers are the most obvious places to find containers, but if you keep your eyes open, you will be surprised not only at what you find to use, but where you find it. All you need to remember is the primary function of the container: to help maintain your plant's root system in a healthy state. Anything built of a nontoxic material which will do this, qualifies, providing it is also durable where you live.

other possible
containers

In selecting containers, keep in mind that there is no law which says they all have to look alike. In your living room you have big chairs and little, fancy chairs and plain. The possibilities for containers are limited only by your own taste, imagination, terrace size, and purse, not necessarily in that order.

Among the more unusual tubs I have found, for example, is one of eucalyptus, held together by bands of bamboo. At the time of purchase, I was so nervous about its potential durability that I only bought one, sort of as an experiment. But the nurseryman was telling the truth and those "delicate" bamboo ties have already outlasted the steel bands on some of my other tubs.

Steel bands which are subject to rust, by the way, can be a problem. It is possible, however, to protect them with rust-inhibiting paint, and at least one New York City nursery, Farm & Garden, will reband planters for a nominal fee.

rust

Another unusual group of plant containers have what might be considered a "lifetime guarantee" (albeit, unwritten). These are manufactured by the Rosenwach Water Tank Co. of 96 North Ninth Street, Brooklyn, N.Y. 11211. Mr. Rosenwach (whose hobby is gardening, of course) realized one day that the wood left over from the construction of his water tanks could be put to excellent use for plants, especially when combined with the principles of tank building. Although these beautiful "Lovable Tubs" (that's what he calls them!) are rather expensive, they surely are durable. If you'd like one, but can't find them at your garden center, write the company for a free brochure.

"lovable tubs?"

I am especially partial to old oak brewery barrels. I like both the clean and shiny ones as well as those which have not yet been "finished." One large barrel which I got directly from a brewery continued to smell strongly of brandy for the entire first summer. I regarded this as a good joke, but I did wonder what the neighbors thought every time the wind shifted. (The tree planted in it showed not the slightest sign of inebriation.)

brewery barrels

While it is important to have a safe, minimum container size for all winter-hardy outdoor plants in cold climates, no summer terrace is complete without pots of colorful flowers or the rich foliage of houseplants, tropicals, and, of course, vegetables and herbs. For them, at that time, there is no such thing as a "minimum" container. I've seen many of

warm-weather pots

these smaller plants growing most happily in teapots, discarded automobile tires, antique urns and Ming vases, whatever it was the owners had to spare. The only problem with some of these possibilities is that one is unable to cut a hole for drainage.

In small containers for these warm weather plants, drainage holes can occasionally be omitted if you are *very* careful with watering (keep it out of the rain) and if a generous layer of rocks is provided at the bottom to help drain excess moisture from the soil (discussed further in the next section).

"tender" plants
outside

Many houseplants are tropical in origin, as noted previously, and in locales subject to cold winters their roots will not survive freezing temperatures outside no matter how big the container. These plants will love a summer vacation on your terrace but do not belong there when the frost comes.

As discussed before, terrace owners can be extremely flexible in their garden plans. And periodically you may choose to move something.

Smaller containers are easy enough to slide or rotate, but an extremely large one cannot be moved so easily. As with some other problems discussed later, you can turn for help with this to the methods used by bonsai gardeners. I don't know if they "invented" the system, but there seems to be a

moving heavy
containers

traditional technique for using rollers and boards to move their large specimens.

First, the container is raised sufficiently on one side to push a board underneath. Then, a second board is pushed under the other side. Next, the boards are raised enough to wedge at least 3 rollers beneath them, either wooden dowels or large metal pipes. (I use old broom handles.)

It is then possible to push the container along on top of these rollers, taking the one which is left behind and transferring it to the front, as one goes along. This is hardly a task to be undertaken alone or too often but it will help you to move your heavy plants when you must.

container or plant first

I regard the question of which to get first, the container or the plant, sort of like asking about the "chicken or the egg." In the case of built-in masonry planters the container frequently comes first. But if you expect to use individual ready-mades, all things are possible.

If you see a container you like, and know you have the room for it somewhere, then buy it and find a suitable plant later.

Conversely, if you see a plant you must have first and know you have the conditions and space for it, then buy it and get a suitable container later. Most nurseries will agree to hold a purchase (as long as you've paid) for a reasonable period which should give you sufficient time to work any way you choose. Quite a flexible system is possible and I believe that really is the nicest way to run a terrace garden.

WORKMEN REMOVED THIS BRICK PLANTER LESS THAN ONE YEAR AFTER THIS PHOTOGRAPH WAS TAKEN. LEAKS IN THE APARTMENT BELOW COULD NOT BE REPAIRED ANY OTHER WAY

A BRICK PLANTER WITH A HONEY-LOCUST TREE AND EUONYMUS SHRUBS LINES THE TERRACE EDGE. A LIGHTER WEIGHT WOOD PLANTER WITH A DWARF JAPANESE MAPLE DIVIDES THE CENTER AREA

IF YOU
BUILD YOUR
OWN, DON'T
FORGET THE
DRAINAGE
HOLES

THESE
PLANTERS ON
A
RECTANGULAR
TERRACE GIVE
THE ILLUSION
OF A CIRCULAR
SPACE. THE
CENTER OF
INTEREST IS A
BLUE
"ATLAS" CEDAR
TREE

AN ARRAY OF
STORE-BOUGHT
CONTAINERS
PERFECTLY
SUITS THIS
HERB GARDEN

REPLACING
STEEL BANDS
ON AN OLDER
TUB

WINDOW
BOXES ON THE
RAILING ARE A
GOOD HOME
FOR SUMMER
PETUNIAS

THE ADVANTAGE
OF HOMEMADE
PLANTERS:
THEY FIT
DIFFICULT
SPOTS PERFECTLY

INDIVIDUAL
TUBS OF
PRIVETS AND
GERANIUMS
DOT THIS
LARGE, WINDY
ROOFTOP

A BRICK
EDGING MARKS
THE PERIPHERY
OF THIS
PLANTING
AREA. THE
SINGLE LARGE
TUB WITH A
CRAB-APPLE
TREE IS
SURROUNDED
BY POTS OF
HOUSEPLANTS,
ROCKS,
GRAVEL, AND A
RECIRCULAT-
ING FOUNTAIN

AN AWNING
OR THE "ROOF"
ABOVE IS
USEFUL FOR
HANGING
SMALL
CONTAINERS
SUCH AS THIS
PLASTIC ONE
WITH
TRADESCANTIA

A
LIGHTWEIGHT
FIBERGLASS
CONTAINER
WITH
FLOWERING
IMPATIENS HAS
THE
APPEARANCE
OF A HEAVY
CONCRETE POT

IN COLD
CLIMATES
HARDY PLANTS
LIKE THESE
RHODODEN-
DRONS DEPEND
ON THEIR
LARGE
CONTAINERS
TO HELP THEM
SURVIVE
OUTDOORS ALL
YEAR LONG

ROOF PIPES IN
THE MIDDLE
OF YOUR
GARDEN
NEEDN'T
DISCOURAGE
YOU. BUILD A
PLANTER
AROUND THEM
AND USE THEM
FOR SUMMER
VINES

NO CONTAINER
WAS NEEDED
AT ALL FOR
THESE SEDUM
PLANTS ON A
PENTHOUSE.
THEY GREW
ROOTS IN THE
SOOT WHICH
FELL BETWEEN
THE GRAVEL

A
"STRAWBERRY
JAR" WITH NO
STRAWBERRIES,
BUT CASCADES
OF HELIOTROPE
AND LOBELIA

A spark in the sun,
this tiny flower has roots
deep in the cool earth.
Harry Behn

Section 5

Happiness Is Planting in Good Soil

dirt is not soil

Contrary to the popular belief of city slickers, "dirt" is not "soil."

Dirt is the stuff on your window sills and under the rug. Soil is what plants have their roots in . . . and there is a big difference.

The basic element of a healthy terrace garden (and, therefore, a happy gardener) is the *original* soil mixed for the containers. There are some plants which are positively neurotic about the composition of their soil. But the majority of trees and shrubs you are likely to encounter have a good tolerance range and manage to adapt. Therefore, while a degree in both chemistry and botany would certainly be useful, it is also possible for the beginner to start with an "all-purpose soil mix" which will be satisfactory. This basic "recipe" need

a basic soil
recipe

not be complex and might read as follows:

> I PART TOPSOIL
>
> I PART SOIL CONDITIONER
>
> I PART LIGHTENER
>
> Mix above dry ingredients together
>   very well.
>
> Add several generous handfuls
>   dehydrated cow manure (optional,

but adds zest and flavor).
Mix well again.

Let's look closer at the ingredients used in the beginner's all-purpose soil mix.

the topsoil   First, about one-third of our total consists of a "topsoil" which must be of good quality. This soil is *not* to be acquired by digging up the nearest park! Aside from the fact that our parks are too valuable to be subjected to such abuse, the soil you find there probably will not be the "topsoil" you need: rich in nutrients plus crumbly in texture.
Instead, the soil you want may be found in the nearest garden center packed in 50- or 100-pound bags. I have reached the point where I can tote a 50-pound load myself . . . but for the novice, not yet used to such exertion, it is better to have these bags delivered directly.

Next, mixed into the recipe, also roughly one-third of the total, is a substance called a soil conditioner. This is any partially decayed organic material.

the soil conditioner   Conditioners supply additional richness to the soil while they continue to decay. In addition, they promote a granular texture and increase the water-holding property of the soil. Gardeners with a yard have a wide choice of conditioners, such as compost, decayed grass clippings, leaf mold, and the like. These items are rather at a premium for most of us in apartments, so another practical conditioner, one easily found at garden centers, is sphagnum peat moss. It comes neatly packed in small lightweight bags, all ready to carry home and use. (It's helpful to moisten it slightly before mixing it into the other ingredients.)

The final major ingredient in this basic recipe is the soil lightener, again roughly one-third total mix.

soil lighteners

Lighteners are inert materials which help increase the porosity of the soil and facilitate the penetration of water and air. Soil lighteners are rock derivatives such as sand, perlite, or vermiculite. Perlite and vermiculite are available at garden centers and both are easy to carry. Perlite may be difficult to work with on windy days as it's so light it flies about. Nevertheless, I prefer it to vermiculite for its greater ability to resist compaction.

In any case, sand is a poor choice for upstairs terraces, primarily because it is heavy and these gardens and gardeners need no additional loads if they can be avoided.

a dash of manure

Finally, for that extra bit of "flavor" stir in several generous handfuls of dehydrated cow manure for each tub batch mixed. Small bags of this excellent natural fertilizer already "deodorized"(?) may also be found at garden centers. I can't guarantee the actual degree of "deodorization" . . . not since the time I spent a hot, sunny afternoon in a car with a package on the seat beside me . . . However, manure is good for the plants and the aroma has the additional quality of evoking nostalgic thoughts of the countryside (real or imagined). Many gardeners eventually come to feel it is not all disagreeable and you know you've "arrived" when you actually begin to like it!

soil structure

The structure of the final soil mix is of extreme importance to the ultimate health of the roots and therefore the entire plant and your garden. This dry mix should have a granular crumb-like feeling which is neither too dense nor full of clods, nor too porous. We want a soil which is "friable" or spongy, the ultimate in soil textures. In any case, don't be afraid to touch it. Pick it up and run it through your fingers.

The goal is to achieve a soil which permits water to penetrate easily, yet not so rapidly that it immediately drains out the bottom of the container.

soil porosity   A delay of several minutes is a good sign.

The beginner should probably test a batch of his first soil mix with a gallon or two of water. I must warn you that this may be a messy experiment but is worth the trouble.

If the water goes through very quickly, more conditioner and some topsoil will be required. If the water takes very long, more than several minutes, then the lightener must be increased.

However, do *not* attempt to correct the structure while the soil is soggy wet. Bothersome as it will be, you should wait until the soil is mostly dry again before making these corrections. Working soil which is very wet and muddy may actually ruin it. Experience will eventually teach you to recognize the feeling of a good dry structure and this messy water experiment may never have to be repeated.

watch those workmen   If you have hired workmen to do the preparation and planting for you, watch them carefully to see that the final soil mix is satisfactory. I learned the hard way that sometimes such workers— good-natured though they may be—often do not understand the importance of the soil and are apt to be careless.

Several years ago I lost a beautiful (not to mention expensive) specimen dwarf tree because its roots could not penetrate the exceedingly compact soil in the tub in which it had been planted. It was too late when I realized that I should have watched their activity and not just assumed that the workmen knew what they were doing when they mixed the soil for this tree.

In recent years there have been experiments in

"soilless" gardening. In some of these cases, perlite
or vermiculite is combined with peat moss only
and the "topsoil" is omitted altogether. This is a
common practice in commercial greenhouses since it
is cheaper to ship "soilless" potted plants which are
very light in weight. Apparently then, this idea is
useful for a gardener who fears excessive weight
loads on his balcony. But in "soilless" mixtures many
chemicals are needed to provide the missing
nutrients plants require. Nothing replaces the
beneficial action of the natural microorganisms
which normally make their home in healthy soil. As
Dr. Charles E. Kellogg, former head of the
National Soil Survey, USDA, says: "An essential
feature of soil is living organisms. No life, no soil."
Because of the construction safety margin written
into newer apartment building codes, it is
unnecessary to completely eliminate the heavy
topsoil in the containers. But for gardens on older
buildings or where a great many large plants are to
be used it is possible to lighten the weight
considerably by *reducing* the proportion of the
topsoil used. According to horticulturist Al
Nordheden, if at least 10 percent soil is retained in
the total mixture, it will still function as the
necessary "essential feature." Thus the recipe
would read, *one* part topsoil to *ten* parts of the peat
and perlite combined.

Another way to deal with a possible weight
problem is to distribute the total load of the
container over a greater floor area. This is done
quite simply by placing it on a larger platform.
One of the best-run roof gardens I have seen was
on top of a very old brownstone. Its dozens of large
container plants were safely resting on such a
decking, which in this case also served as a
protective flooring entirely covering the roof.

When working with trees and shrubs which are
B & B or container-grown, it is possible to plant
virtually any time of the year. And many suburban
gardeners with yards do. But I have found that on

when to plant

terraces, the only really good time to plant large
woody plants is in the spring, for several reasons.
First, if the terrace is subject to severe winter winds
and the plant has not had time to develop anchoring
roots, it might very well disappear with the first
strong gust. This could be avoided, of course, if
you go to the added trouble and expense of tying it
down . . . but why bother?
For in any case, the chance of winter survival is
reduced if the fine feeder roots which absorb the
nutrients and water even during dormancy are not
well developed.
Thus, it is better in cold climate areas to plant in the
spring just before the growing period begins, so
that by the following winter the plant is sufficiently
established to survive.

preparing the
mix

While planting should take place only in the spring,
preparing the soil mix may be done nearly any time.
The only prerequisite is that the topsoil be neither
muddy wet nor frozen. Many garden books advocate
preparing soil as much as a season ahead of the
actual planting (like making a stew and letting it
sit for a while). This is a good idea, especially if you
intend to do a lot of planting all at once. It is much
easier to have the tubs already filled so that all you
have to do is put the plants in. This requires enough
energy for one day as it is.
But while this may be ideal, things rarely work out
this way and the soil mixing and the planting are
often done at the same time. This is because the soil,
as well as the plant, is store-bought and invariably
the two are delivered together. (Gardeners with
yards *have* the soil to begin with and need only to

improve its quality for planting.)

One big headache, however, is to find a place in which to mix the soil and then, solving that, to find a place in which to store whatever is left over. Some terrace owners do this by setting aside a large plastic garbage pail or box for both the mixing and storing.

I prefer to work tub by tub, mixing only the amount of soil I need at the time. I do this either in the container itself after the drainage layer is in (to be discussed next), right on the terrace floor, or on a large plastic sheet. Whatever mix is left over after my planting is done, I dump into a heavy polyethylene bag and hide (more or less) in a corner.

keep what's
left over

In the past, rather than attempting to store the left-over mix, I used to give it away. But I found that I often wound up regretting this generosity, since not long after I would once again be needing more for myself.

In any event, when to prepare the soil mix is of less importance than how to prepare the container. And as the planting of a plant is from the bottom up, that is precisely where we shall now begin.

there's more
than soil in
that tub

A basic requirement of a healthy plant is a healthy root system. The success of that system depends primarily on the *drainage* or the amount of water remaining around the roots. Few plants do well with continually "wet feet" . . . and you may be sure that home owners with poor garden soil drainage suffer untold agonies in attempting to correct the problem. Yet how easy it is for us to avoid this difficulty in the first place! Our "planting" starts with the placing of a drainage layer. Materials typically used for this are pebbles, rocks, marble chips, broken flowerpots (crock), or any rough, inert material which permits the easy flow of water.

This layer, placed first on the bottom of the
container, may vary from about 1½ inches for
smaller tubs up to about 3 inches or so for really tall
planters. But while the water is encouraged to drain
out, the rest of the tub's contents must not and we
can prevent this by covering the holes at the
bottom of the container with pieces of rounded,
broken flowerpots (or broken soup bowls) with
their curved side up.

After the drainage layer is in place, it is a good idea
to add a screen of fiberglass, or a thin layer of
rough-textured moss (not peat moss) to help keep
the soil mix in place and prevent its sneaking out
past the drainage pebbles. One terrace gardener I
know, uses several sheets of newspaper for this, with
apparently satisfactory results. The roots of the
plants, once established, prevent this movement of
soil just as they do on hillsides. But since it will be
a while before enough rootlets develop, you may
have a muddy mess on the floor when you water if
you omit the screening material.

Once the drainage layer and screen are in place,
add your soil mix if it is already prepared or carefully
add all the ingredients and do the mixing right in
the tub. Mix enough to fill the tub about
three-quarters full, leaving a "hole" for the plant's
root ball. While important to do properly,
preparing the container is really as simple as that
and the principle will be familiar to anyone who
has worked with houseplants.

Although the idea is the same, it is on a much
larger scale and the terrace gardener, especially the
city dweller, who is in poor physical condition may
be overwhelmed. Mixing large quantities of soil, or
planting a large plant, can be extremely demanding.
But taken slowly, it could be just what the doctor
might order.

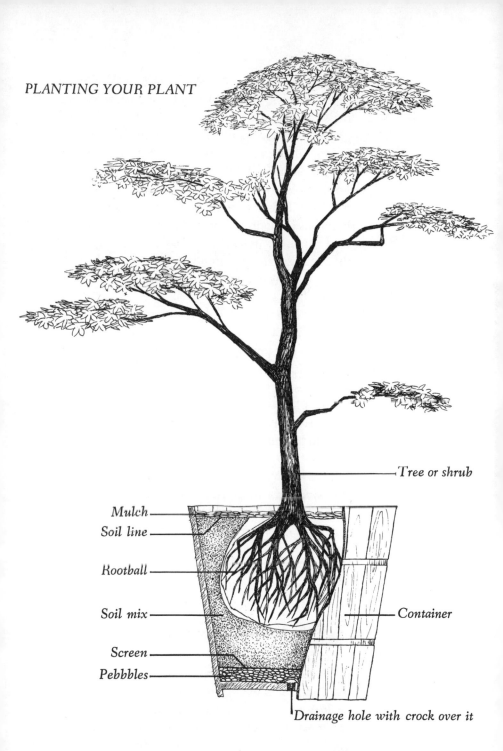

PLANTING YOUR PLANT

Tree or shrub

Mulch

Soil line

Rootball

Soil mix

Screen

Pebbbles

Container

Drainage hole with crock over it

To plant a tree or shrub which is nursery-delivered as B & B stock, lift the plant up supporting the root mass from *below*. The natural tendency will be to grasp it by its trunk and let the root ball hang. Try to avoid doing this as you may tear small roots.

planting b & b
stock

Set the entire ball directly into the "hole" you have left for it and position the plant however you wish it to face. This is your chance to start those spreading branches going in the right direction! Then, cut the cord which encircles the root ball and gently loosen the topmost burlap. Cut away as much of the burlap as you can easily undo *without upsetting the main root ball*.

Natural burlap eventually disintegrates and is sufficiently porous that the roots will grow right through; thus, many ground-level gardeners remove none of it. But I remove as much as I can easily get at because the containers are so limited in size that I would rather use every bit of space for good soil.

removing the
burlap

If the tree has been wrapped in a synthetic fabric (a common practice recently) it is especially important to remove as much as possible . . . so long as it can be done without disturbing or breaking those roots. Remember at all times that you have paid a premium price for a plant with a good root mass completely intact. It is up to you to keep it that way when you plant it.

In the case of a plant which is in a nursery container of metal, the sides should have been cut for you at the shop. If not, you can attempt to do this yourself. But lacking a set of metal shears, do not ruin any of your garden tools by using them for this purpose.

stock in metal
nursery
containers

The alternative is to slip the specimen out of its pot just as you would an ordinary houseplant. This is done by carefully turning the container upside down while holding your open hand flat against the earth surrounding the plant's base. (To prevent a loss of soil.) If the shrub is large, this won't be easy and so another method is to lay the container on its side, preferably on a large sheet (plastic or otherwise). Using a hammer, sharply rap the *top* rim of the container all around. It should then be easy to slide the container off. Using the sheet as a support for the root mass and soil, gently lift the plant into its new home. Again try to work in such a way that the entire root mass and fine rootlets stay together as much as possible.

stock in plantable nursery containers

Sometimes a plant comes in a container made of cardboard with printed directions that it is not to be removed. Quite often this is done with plants such as roses where the roots have been trimmed severely and may not yet be redeveloped. The soil in such containers has been specially mixed to help the plant's development and frequently the container is the only reason why the whole thing is staying together. Therefore, plant the container in its entirety, following all of the grower's instructions carefully.

adding soil around the root ball

Once the plant is in position, fill the remaining open area in the tub with your soil mix, patting or tamping down carefully but firmly to eliminate large air pockets. Dr. Stephen Tim of the Brooklyn Botanic Garden suggests that this may be done most effectively with a flat piece of wood. The soil line around the trunk must not be higher than it was in the field where the plant was originally grown. You can tell where this level should be if you study the base of the trunk and see where the dry woody part begins. The idea is to avoid either raising or lowering this soil line. To do so may cause decay or vulnerability to parasites, respectively.

This point and thus the final level of the soil

should be about 2 inches *below* the rim of your container. This will make watering later much easier and prevent the soil from washing over the tub's top. But the main reason for saving these last 2 inches is to leave room for adding the final layer in the tub: a mulch.

the importance
of a mulch

A mulch is a protective soil surface covering used to reduce the caking and crusting caused by the elements. Mulches also help to stabilize the temperature of the soil, aid in retaining moisture at the root level, and inhibit the growth of weeds which rob plants of vital nutrients.
The ground-level gardener must deal with these problems too, but in a container on an upstairs terrace they become intensified. So while some gardeners may choose to have a mulch covering their gardens at certain times of the year only, for container plants there are incalculable advantages to using one all year round.

typical mulch
materials

Materials useful for mulching are as different from each other as the personalities of the gardeners themselves. Possibilities include a disparate range of objects such as pieces of bark, fallen leaves, coffee grounds, cocoa bean shells, sawdust, cat litter, bird cage cleanings, white marble chips, plastic sheeting, and even pages from the New York *Times* (political view notwithstanding). Any and all of these are useful, legitimate mulches, bizarre as some may sound. The question then is which mulch should you choose?

choosing a
mulch

Since it is important periodically to rework the soil in the tubs, it is a distinct advantage to select something which may easily be pushed aside or at least may be of some benefit if later mixed into the soil. Good gardening practice advocates using mulches which help restore nutrients at the same time they protect, but this is not always possible for us. Quite frequently some of the best ground-level mulches are very light in weight and wind up on the floor when used in windy upstairs gardens. Depending on your conditions, this may immediately eliminate sawdust, grass, hay, and peat moss. (Peat moss, in addition to flying around a lot at first, also cakes rather badly when wet and is rarely a good mulch even on the ground, despite what some books say.)

On the other hand, a layer of even the prettiest little white marble chips or seashells can present some annoying problems when accidentally mixed into the soil.

Thus, while I absolutely suggest experimenting with anything which appeals to you, I have found that medium-size bark chips are the most practical for terrace use. They will not fly away in the wind, and may easily be moved to rework the tub. If they are mixed into the soil accidentally, although their rate of decay is quite slow, they are eventually "decayable," which is more than I can say for rocks. Do wear gloves while working with bark mulch, as they can yield tiny, very nasty splinters.

working with mulches

In the larger tubs, it is also quite useful to add a layer of newspaper strips, 2 or 3 pages thick, *under* whatever mulch is used. Newspaper is particularly good for keeping weeds to a minimum (especially near the bird feeders) and disintegrates sufficiently to be reworked into the soil when the time comes to cultivate. After reading world events, I feel a lot better when I remember that the newspaper at least benefits my plants.

newspaper strips

For a number of years, I struggled in my upstairs garden using only a small hand trowel and fork. While these are the basic tools required by any

basic tools for
soil work gardener, my prejudices as a city dweller were such
that the idea of owning anything larger seemed
ridiculous. I even met a fellow balcony owner who
used only a big kitchen spoon.
But one day after I had acquired more large
containers, I found myself in a garden center staring
at a long-handled shovel with a very narrow blade
(that's the digging part). Suddenly I knew what
I had been missing in life.
For unless your balcony is really tiny or you have
limited yourself to window boxes only, a long-
handled shovel is a most useful instrument, indeed.
And for the soil cultivation and restoration so
important later on, a long-handled fork is also
helpful.

In addition to these obvious tools for soil work, there
are two items equally useful but often overlooked.
A broom and dustpan!

a broom is
basic After all, the "floor" of our gardens really is just
that. And I can think of no other way to clean up
spilled soil . . . than with a broom. I have a special
plastic set exclusively for outdoor use. And that is
just where I keep them. Since I am really a nut on
keeping my garden neat, I also use a mop on the
floor outside, swabbing away, sailor-style. But the
broom alone will suffice if you are not this fussy.

At this point at the end of your first planting day, after the floor is clean again, you will probably be a total wreck, so the best thing to do is sit back and admire your handiwork.

As soon as you recover, and certainly within the next 12 hours or so, water all newly planted specimens thoroughly. And you now have my sincere congratulations. If you've made it this far you are well along the way to having a wonderful terrace garden.

SOME BASIC
TOOLS FOR
SOIL WORK

BROKEN
FLOWER POTS
ARE USED TO
COVER
DRAINAGE
HOLES

THE DRAINAGE
LAYER IS
COMPOSED OF
SMALL ROCKS
AND BROKEN
POTS

A FIBERGLASS
SCREEN HELPS
PREVENT
MOVEMENT OF
SOIL UNTIL
ROOTS DEVELOP

PREPARING A
GOOD SOIL MIX

THIS ROSE IS
PLANTED
CARDBOARD
BOX AND ALL
AS DIRECTED
ON THE LABEL

LOOSEN THE
BURLAP
AROUND THE
TRUNK OF
B & B STOCK

REMOVE AS
MUCH OF THE
TOP AND SIDE
BURLAP AS
POSSIBLE

ADD SOIL IN
AROUND THE
SIDES,
TAMPING
FIRMLY

AND FINALLY,
THE MULCH
IS ADDED. IN
THIS CASE, IT'S
BARK CHIPS

128

THE WEIGHT OF HEAVY TUBS MAY BE DISTRIBUTED OVER A GREATER AREA THROUGH THE USE OF PLANK PLATFORMS. THESE FLOWERING PERIWINKLES ARE ON SUCH A FLOORING

NEW B & B ARBORVITAE SHRUBS WAIT PATIENTLY TO BE PLANTED

Tomatoes

The falling leaves
fall and pile up; the rain
beats on the rain
Gyōdai

Section 6

Water Is the Staff of Life

To water, and how often to water; this is a most
pondered question!
Unfortunately for the terrace gardener, the subject
appears deceptively simple, so he may fail to realize
it is one of the most important tasks he must assume.
Let us start with the basic question regarding any
garden.
How do you know if your plants need water?
The late Louis Politi, when queried thus by his
classes at The New York Botanical Garden, would
reply:

> "Don't be afraid to ruin your
> manicure! Stick your fingers into the
> soil and find out how wet it is!"

And I cannot beat this for accuracy or succinctness.

how to water

In general, all plants need a thorough, deeply
penetrating watering, generous enough for the
entire root ball. The word *deep* is important. (As I
occasionally remind the porters who tend the trees
in front of our building: "Put enough water into
the soil to reach the very *top* of the tree!") The
majority of plants then prefer to reach a nearly dry
state before the entire deep watering process is
repeated.

When purchasing a tree or shrub, investigate if it
falls into this "majority" category or if it is at one of
the water preference extremes. There are a few
plants such as willows or some ferns, which must
have their roots wet at all times. These plants are
the ones whose natural state is close to streams or
within the denseness of a forest. In addition, many
summer fruits or vegetables such as cucumbers and
tomatoes require a great deal of water to develop
properly.

know your
plants'
preferences

At the other extreme are the plants which prefer
more arid conditions and cannot stand having "wet
feet" between waterings. These plants often have
thick fleshy stems or leaves and retain a good deal
of moisture for varying periods of time. This group,
which may even benefit from a little neglect,
includes cacti and others known as succulents.
If several plants are to be grouped in a single
container, it is logical that they should have the
same general water tolerance.

There is an old wives' tale which insists that plants
must "never be watered in full sun." As with all
such stories, there is a little bit of fact and a lot of
fiction in this and so it produces heated discussions
among amateur gardeners.

what time to
water

Remember that the goal at all times is a deeply
penetrating watering. If every day the terrace
gardener appears promptly at high noon and lightly
sprinkles the parched soil, this is not a deep
watering. The roots will begin to grow toward the
miserly amount of moisture found only up top. If
this process occurs repeatedly, those roots will
eventually surface sufficiently to be burned by the
sun and the plant will weaken and die. Substance
will thus be given to the statement about not
watering in midday.

But if the water is properly administered, and fully penetrates the entire root ball, there will be no reason for the roots to grow toward the surface.

If they are down where they belong it won't matter how strong the sun is, so the time of day won't matter and the watering can be done at the gardener's own convenience.

However, there is no general information being passed around about the possible danger of watering in the evening. And this is really the time to avoid such activity. As darkness falls, the food-making processes slow. With the sun gone there is no immediate need for a great deal of water and the roots remain soggy for many hours. This is ideal for the growth of fungi and bacteria, and so it is an invitation to trouble to repeatedly do all your watering as night falls.

With regard to predicting the water needed, you must know what is really happening on your particular terrace. As discussed in the second section, it is only by direct observation that you become familiar with the small climatic conditions present in your garden.

wind and sun
dehydration

The wind and sun are hot and drying in the summer . . . and cold and drying in the winter. These forces are present in varying degrees all the time on many terraces. This externally caused dehydration is different from that resulting from the normal food-making process of the plants, but the plant's need for water may be just as great. Thus you may find that a plant located at one end of your terrace will require much more (or much less) water than if the same plant were located at the other end. You don't have to move the plant but do water according to this need.

The next important factor affecting water

requirements is the container.

Here, the gardener with trees and shrubs planted

container
moisture loss in the ground definitely has an easier time of it. The roots of his plants are free to seek water in areas other than immediately at their base. It is not unusual, for example, to find roots of mature trees dozens of yards away from their trunk.

A light summer rain, then, may afford some moisture benefit to a ground-level garden. But it is totally inadequate for the terrace garden. And, while a good deal of moisture from a heavy rainfall will be retained in the soil of a garden planted in the ground, in containers the excess moisture will evaporate from the sides as well as leach out the bottom.

Thus, unlike your country counterpart, you may well need to water again, very soon.

drainage holes It might be tempting at this point to consider using containers without any drainage holes, to overcome this problem. But this will result in stagnant water at the bottom of the containers which will suffocate the roots and encourage the growth of undesirable microorganisms which cause rot. So this is one idea which should be discarded immediately, certainly in the case of large trees and shrubs. (In Section 4 mention is made of omitting drainage holes in some of the small pots, but precautions must be taken when watering such plants, and they cannot be permitted out in the rain, etc.)

overwatering Which brings us to the question of overwatering. I should like to reiterate the importance of a proper soil structure and the drainage layer and container holes as factors in maintaining proper moisture levels (see Section 5). But generally speaking it is the rare terrace tree or shrub which dies of overwatering. Certainly if you remember to *touch* your soil to feel how wet, it is easy to avoid any problem in this area. And in view of the numerous dehydrating factors present outside, the type of improper overwatering which leads to houseplant death indoors hardly ever occurs.

On the contrary . . . the problem outside usually is one of insufficient water. Several consecutive, really hot summer days no matter the apparent weakness of wind or sun may be the beginning of the end for an unwatered terrace tree or shrub.

small plants on small balconies

Most terrace gardeners like to give their houseplants an outdoor summer vacation. In the case of small balconies in particular, houseplants outside are a delight, especially when combined with annuals, producing a minute, colorful garden. But this array of tiny containers outside can produce watering chores of unbelievable proportions on hot days. Where possible, group these small pots together within a single larger container. Such a container might be a tray on the floor or a window box hung on the railing. The little pots can then be surrounded with soil or sphagnum moss to further reduce moisture loss.

Where the houseplants are too large for this, catch saucers of generous soup-dish size can be used to retain the runoff water.

In any case, the small plants should be grouped close together and each will benefit from the other as moisture evaporates from the leaves.

faucetless gardens

As an economy measure for construction companies, high-rise apartment building terraces are sometimes built without water faucets. (I myself have yet to have one equipped with an outdoor faucet.) This means that the determined gardener is forced through his living room with pitchers of water for thirsty plants. Each terrace owner with this problem must soon decide how he wishes to solve it, for in an effort to save himself some work, he may water a little less than he should!

water equipment

One solution is to use a lightweight plastic watering pail of two-gallon capacity. This is the ideal size and is readily available as well. A pail of less than two gallons means excessive trips back and forth. More than two gallons may be too heavy for the average person to carry and will be difficult, if not impossible, to fill from the kitchen or bathroom source. One consolation, however, is that you will be able to use tepid tap water, which on a hot day is better for your plants anyway.

But, outdoor faucet or not, no matter how tiny the balcony, if there are a reasonable number of plants to be looked after, it is far better to buy a *hose*. Lightweight 25- or 50-foot, small-diameter hoses are available at many city hardware or 5 & 10¢ stores and make life a lot easier. Buy a hose of good quality, as the very cheap ones tend to kink quite easily . . . a habit which is extremely annoying, to say the least.

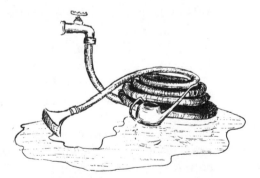

If there is no outside faucet, you can purchase appropriate adapters for connecting the hose to your kitchen or bathroom sink. First, check the exact size and position of the threads on the faucet you plan to use. If no hose connection will screw on directly, you can buy a gadget made by the Melard Mfg. Co., called a "snap coupler" at a hardware or plumbing supply store. This will do the job.

The hose may then be run out through the nearest terrace window or door. This simplifies the watering task to merely running back and forth to modulate water pressure and temperature. But it is still better than working only with a watering pail.

The hose can also be used for cleaning the terrace floor, the windows, the outside furniture, and, of course, the plants.

That's right, cleaning the plants.

The city especially is a dirty, sooty place and if you notice that your window sills get dirty, you may notice that your plants do too. (Fortunately, it's less noticeable.) It's important to remember that plants are living things and are "breathing" through their leaves. In the food manufacturing process of photosynthesis, they absorb carbon dioxide through the stomata or microscopic openings on their leaves or needles and return oxygen to the atmosphere.

If the leaves are coated with layers of city soot and dirt not only will they be unable to perform this vital task, but the available *light* will be reduced as well. Aside from the eventual faltering of your own individual plants, consider for a moment what this will lead to throughout the Earth itself.

Therefore, keep your plants clean!

A weekly, forceful hosing of *both* the upper and lower leaf surfaces not only keeps your plants clean, but will have the additional benefit of helping keep unwanted pests to a minimum. Furthermore, if the weather is very hot, dry, or windy, many plants will make use of the added moisture on their leaves, during the day.

I do believe that if more people cleaned their trees and shrubs periodically (and this includes houseplants), then more plants would survive the rigors of city life.

There is some speculation about water on plant leaves causing burns in strong sunlight. For trees and shrubs there appears to be little truth to this. But it has been established that water which remains on the leaves for extended periods, especially at night, may induce undesirable bacterial or fungus development in some species. As I said before, with regard to watering in general, keep those nighttime cleanings to a minimum, especially if there's no wind.

As the days in fall shorten, the plants slowly enter a period of rest or dormancy. This means they are going to sleep, not dying.

don't forget the fall and spring

As deciduous trees and shrubs begin to lose their leaves, water requirements decrease. But *some moisture is still needed* and continues to be, all winter long.

As the days in early spring begin to lengthen, the plants enter a period of active growth and the need for moisture starts to increase. All too often, terrace trees and shrubs suffer serious damage during this time simply because their owner is not aware that they must have some moisture. Gardens in the ground often retain enough water between rains to sustain them during this time. But terrace plants are not so fortunate.

seasonal decreasing and increasing water requirements

As the fall progresses, I permit my plants to go for longer and longer periods without water. I supplement what may have come from above but permit the tubs to remain dry for several days in between. This is very different from midsummer,

138

when extended periods of dryness can be disastrous. The frequency of my watering continues to taper off still more as the cold of winter descends. Once all the leaves are gone, I stop watering nearly completely. Later, as the winter becomes spring and the days begin to lengthen, so the frequency of my watering slowly increases.

Unfortunately, it is not possible for me to state exactly "how often" these waterings should be done. As in the summer, the determining factors will be the temperature of the air during the day, the amount of sun, the strength of the winds, the container's size, and plant preference.

And of course, what has or has not come from above.

midwinter
waterings

Just as the terrace gardener realizes the uselessness of a light summer shower for his garden, he may also realize the equally useless effects of light winter snow or rain. If mild midwinter temperatures cause deep thawing of the soil and if there is little snow or rain, then the terrace gardener has to compensate for nature's lack. He must try to notice and remember how much moisture nature may have supplied over an extended period (about a month or so) and determine its adequacy for his own terrace's conditions and plants. For example, winter needs of evergreens are greater than those of deciduous trees and shrubs.

His friends may think he's nuts, but the terrace owner *occasionally* has to water some or all of his plants right in the middle of winter.

how to water
in the cold

The best time for midwinter watering is early on a day when the temperature is expected to remain well above freezing. This minimizes the possibility of the water freezing too quickly to be of benefit to the plant or causing damage to the roots. Don't use your plastic hose during the cold weather since it's likely to crack, and, indeed, it should be taken indoors in late fall. Since not all the tubs will require winter water, it shouldn't be too difficult to handle it with the big watering can. If you use water from inside the apartment (outside faucets often are inoperable), use cold water only. Remember that although the frequency of watering may alter considerably now, the principle of a deep and thorough watering does not.

making use of fallen snow

Sometimes it is possible to cope in advance with supplemental winter watering by making use of any snow which may have fallen on the floor. I have convinced my children that it is great fun to shovel all the snow up onto the tree tubs. Such snow first provides a mulch-like insulating layer. As it melts, it supplies the water at the right time. Several years ago, Max Berg, founder of the Farm and Garden Nursery in Manhattan, informed me that snow was known as the "poor man's mulch" long before I discovered its advantages.

Owners of balconies which are in tiers, and thus covered from above, must take special note of nature's lack not only in the summer but throughout the entire year. In the summer, the plants' need for water will be obvious. The rain may fall but the balcony floor remains dry and the flowers droop from lack of water.

balconies with roofs

But as the annuals fade and the shrubs drop their leaves and enter their dormant period, the tiered-balcony owner can easily forget that the roof over his plants also prevents the snow from reaching them. With no wilting petunias around to remind him, he may be unaware of his shrubs' or trees' continuing need for moisture.

When I was the owner of such a sheltered garden, two consecutive winters (or was it autumns and springs, too?) of losing expensive plants finally taught me that I should have watered them all year long!

A difficult problem confronts the terrace owner who must be away for an extended period during the growing season. Who will water the plants? Depending on the length of his absence and the size of the containers, he may consider leaving them in nature's care. But for extended periods this will not afford much peace of mind. It is usually better to find a willing and responsible friend nearby who will accept the privilege of enjoying the garden in return for watering the plants.
At such a time, it is wise to take hanging plants down, group all the smaller pots together, and give clear instructions about which plants like lots of water and which can do with less.
The tendency for the uninitiated will be to under water the large tubs. So the importance of thorough watering must be stressed. (I implore my friends to "drown the willow" . . .) If the person is interested in plants, the job of explaining will be minimal and easily understood. But if your friend is not the least interested in the plants and is just trying to be helpful . . . well, you may console yourself with the thought that basically strong plants have good powers of regeneration.

More than one terrace owner, however, has experimented with installing some form of piped watering system. If done improperly, these systems not only are unsightly, but are totally useless, which is worse. Few plumbers understand how to install a watering system in a garden and few country landscape contractors (experienced only with sprinkler systems) understand how to deal with a terrace.

when you're
away

water systems

The problems which arise usually are the result of uneven pressure throughout the system and improper distribution of the water throughout the individual planters.

adapting
nurserymen's
methods

If it is of any consolation, commercial nurserymen too are faced with the enormous task of watering, especially as labor costs rise. Consequently, in recent years several systems have been perfected for these greenhouses which may be adapted by us. Among the most widely used is the Chapin Watermatic System. It entails the installation of a special self-sealing polyvinyl tubing which carries the water to a number of small "spaghetti" feeders plugged into the main line. These, in turn, distribute the water to the containers where needed. While this system is fully automated in commercial greenhouses and it is possible for the terrace owner to install it that way, I prefer to control the watering myself. (If it's raining cats and dogs, the system need not be on as well.) However, for terrace owners who must be away a lot, the automated part sounds like a good idea. In areas where winter damage may occur it is wise to drain the lines before the deep cold sets in.

Installing the Chapin Watermatic System is relatively inexpensive if you are able to do it yourself. It is available from commercial nursery suppliers, some of whom are willing to deal on a retail basis. One such supplier is Al Saffer & Co. in Manhattan. As noted in Section 4, Al Saffer's catalogue is full of all kinds of goodies for the enthusiastic amateur, even though it is really intended for tradesmen. You can also write the Chapin people directly at P. O. Box 298, Watertown, N.Y. 13601, for additional distributors' names. In any case, automated or not, a good water system on a large terrace, one which really works, is worth every bit of time or money it may cost to have installed.

is it going to rain today?

Just as farmers have done for eons, so the amateur gardener glances at the sky, wondering if the rains will come and save him some work. Several years ago, I decided to splurge on a barometer in order to have an idea of what to expect. The movement of the hand on the dial of a barometer indicates the changes in atmospheric pressure within about a three-hour period. A very rapid rise indicates improvement and fair weather ahead. A very rapid fall means a storm is not far off.

Although the strength and direction of the winds are also necessary factors in properly interpreting the weather, I have found my barometer to be a pretty handy gadget (decorative as well) which gives me some idea of what may happen in the next few hours. The actual amount of rain, I cannot predict. But at least I can plan my gardening day a bit better (and also venture a guess as to whether or not my husband should carry an umbrella).

rain gages

In addition, after years of trying to figure out how to ascertain if enough rain or snow did finally fall, I recently came across an inexpensive tool which solved my problem. Called a "rain and sprinkler gage," it shows the exact amount in calibrated graduations. Modeled on the order of an expensive instrument, this little plastic tube is actually quite cheap and certainly worth its weight in gold. Now, after a summer deluge (or what *appears* to be a deluge) I look out at my little rain gage and know for sure what has happened.

This instrument is called the "Taylor 5-inch Clear-vu Gage" and is available at many garden centers. If you can't find it or something similar

locally, write to the Marketing Department of the
Taylor Instrument Corporation in Arden, North
Carolina 28704, and ask for their catalogue.

Tiny city balcony or huge country estate, proper
watering is one of the most important gardening
tasks. Occasionally it may appear to be only a
bothersome chore but gardeners and farmers
everywhere feel this way sometimes too . . .
You may be assured that steadfastness in this
area will yield rich rewards.

NO OUTSIDE WATER
FAUCET? GET A HOSE
ATTACHMENT
FOR THE
BATHROOM OR
KITCHEN SINK

LARGER
GARDENS
ENJOY THE
LUXURY OF
HOSE REELS

MAKING A
HOLE FOR A
FEEDER LINE
IN A NEWLY
INSTALLED
WATER SYSTEM

A "RAIN GAGE"
TELLS WHAT REALLY
CAME FROM ABOVE,
SOMETIMES IT'S QUITE
DIFFERENT FROM WHAT
YOU MAY HAVE THOUGHT

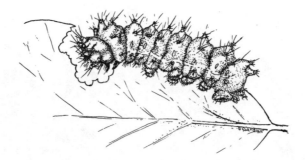

Caterpillar enjoying lunch

"Pests"
The rose-bug on the rose
     Is evil—so are those
          Who see the rose-bug
               Not the rose.
                    Ella M. Boult

Section 7

A Few Problems

City slicker that I am, the thought of sharing my
territory with "bugs" was always a revolting idea.
The word evoked images of repulsive creatures like
cockroaches, silverfish, or mosquitoes . . . horrid
little things which either revel in dirt or make me
scratch. So when the first caterpillar made its
appearance on the terrace, my family was torn
between apprehension and awe of the creature
which we assumed had arrived "on foot" (feet?),
crawling up many floors. Later, when I told a
suburban nurseryman he laughed in disbelief. Not
at the supposed multistory hike, but at the idea that
any such insect life was found in midcity.

a caterpillar on
a skyscraper?

As the plant collection on my terrace increased, the
caterpillars did too , . . along with other beautiful
and fascinating comrades whose entomological
classification would boggle any city dweller's mind.
I started to wonder then not only at the amazing
events evolving before me, but at that nurseryman's
knowledge of city life and "bugs" in general.
It soon became apparent that just because we fail
to see these beings arrive (in one stage or other of
their life cycle), that doesn't mean they don't.
And assumptions about city insects
notwithstanding, they abound here!

Now before we panic into preparing an all-out attack on these (alleged) "enemies" of man, let us think about them for a moment.

There are several *hundred thousand* kinds of insects in North America. Without them, as Dr. Cynthia Westcott says in *The Gardener's Bug Book,* life as we know it could not exist.

We depend on them for pollination of more than three-quarters of our food crops and flowers. In addition to eating each other and holding both the insect and plant population in balance, they are useful as scavengers, food for some birds, fish and animals and important medicinal and commercial products as well.

Thus, the first thing to do when you spy an insect enjoying your garden is look at it carefully and ask yourself, "What is he doing?"

If he appears to be minding his own business and you have no previous evidence that he is in fact a "bad" guy, follow the old American philosophy and *presume innocence till proven guilty.*

when in doubt, leave him alone

When in doubt, leave him alone!

Keep in mind, too, that looks can be misleading; some of man's best friends have a fearsome visage. For example, several times in the last few years I have found the strange, but beneficial, monsters known as praying mantises on my terrace (although my children were frightened at first by the awesome things).

One year a mantis remained with us an entire summer. He (?) alternated between a tub of roses and a tub of marigolds, eating an assortment of fellow insects. By fall, he had become so much a part of our lives that the children decided to give him a name. In retrospect, I can only wonder at city children who can casually call such a "pet" *Bob.*

In addition to praying mantises and ladybugs, there are many other predators in the insect world who spend at least one stage of their metamorphosis dining exclusively on other insects. How many of the following *friends* will you know when they come to your garden?

a list of some friends

ANTLION OR DOODLEBUG
Long soft body with long wings

BANDED THRIPS
Yellow to dark brown, banded or longitudinally striped

CHECKERED BEETLES
Long narrow body covered with dense hairs

DAMSELBUGS
Tiny black or yellowish brown with bent-looking front legs

DRAGONFLIES
Two pairs of long membranous wings with a long extended body which looks like an outstretched tail

EARTHWORMS
Actually tiny animals (you know what these are); they don't eat insects but do help keep the soil aerated

GREEN LACEWING
Has large, delicate-looking wings held upward in a triangular or tent-like position

GROUND BEETLES
Ferocious-looking nocturnal insects,
they are fairly long, generally black
and shiny, with long legs

PARASITIC WASPS
Several varieties of wasps which dine
exclusively on insect prey

SOLDIER BEETLES
Soft bodies, black or brown with
some bright color

SPIDERS
You know what spiders look like . . .
they eat insects, remember?

TACHINID FLIES
Strongly resembling the house fly,
these are larger, more hairy and
bee-like

Pardon the "name-dropping" but I can't resist listing
some friends, a number of which I first met on my
own terrace.
Of the thousands of crawling, flying, burrowing
creatures, the good guys (from man's point of
view) actually outnumber the bad. Can any of us
be so irresponsible then as to wantonly destroy *all*
of these beings just to get rid of an annoying
minority?
It is true that in a tiny garden one cannot maintain
that balance of nature wherein the insects hold each
other in check. Yet if each one of us tries to disturb
this system no more than is absolutely necessary, we
will *all* be rewarded as the collective effort begins to
work. There is no doubt in my mind that there are

times when terrace owners must help keep the pests under control. But it is *unnecessary, unwise,* and *positively dangerous* to blithely splatter insecticides about . . . especially when you don't know what you're doing or why.

Never mind the casual way they're available, sold by salespeople who may be quite ignorant. These things are serious poisons and should only be used *as a last resort.*

	Bug	Beetle	Moth or Butterfly
Egg			
Nymph, Grub or Caterpillar stage			
Resting stage			
Adult			

TYPICAL INSECT LIFE CYCLES

basic pest controls

So, given the possibility that the insect(s) discovered definitely is not a friend, what are some ways of getting rid of it without lethal poisons? The first method guaranteed to discourage an extremely wide range of undesirables is simply a full-force blast of water with your hose! In Section 6, I mentioned washing plants in order to keep them "clean" enough to breathe, so "clean" may now be interpreted any way you wish. (This is especially important for gardeners with automatic watering systems who may never hose their plants' foliage.) This "fireman's welcome" can be repeated on several consecutive days to convince the invaders they really aren't wanted. When a very strong water stream hits (aim in particular at the *undersides* of the leaves), well, they get the hint soon enough.

To prevent possible breakage of any tender growth, support weak stems or flower buds with one hand, while hosing closely with the other. Healthy plants are pretty sturdy, though, and rarely harmed by such water force.

Another way to get rid of some pests when plain water doesn't impress them, is to wash or spray with a solution of very warm water and lots of *soap*. A face full of suds is quite unappetizing and few visitors come back for seconds. Some gardeners have experimented with homemade mixes and come up with reportedly successful insect repellents. The most widely acclaimed is a blend of onions, hot peppers, and garlic, ground well and mixed with a small quantity of water. A spray of finely ground tomato leaves soaked in water is another. (The odor of these sprays may also keep your neighbors away.)

Still another way to control unwanted visitors is simply by "removal." Sanitation is a key weapon in the fight against problems. Those hidden spots behind the tubs and in little corners are perfect breeding grounds for many pests. A minimal cleanup effort may well stop many problems before they begin.

water and
water mixes

removal

It is not difficult to pick off by hand larger beetle or caterpillar pests (or their egg masses or cocoons). At first you may be too squeamish just to throw them on the floor and stomp on them. But with time and hard work, you can attain this advanced level of gardening.

If you prefer, you can knock them into a jar and give them to a school or camp for "nature study." These institutions will be grateful for your altruism and remain unsuspicious of the true nature of your generosity.

The logical extension of "removal" of individual insects is the cutting away of portions of the plant itself. The pruning of parasite-infested limbs is an important method of controlling many pests as well as diseases. In her books, Dr. Westcott urges gardeners to "carry a large paper bag" for the express purpose of readily removing afflicted remains.

varied
plantings

Many plant-eating pests have definite likes and dislikes which we can also use to advantage. It is not uncommon, for example, to watch a plant being devoured leafless while one right next to it is completely ignored by the little beasts. Since it is easier to control pests on a single plant, if you have varied your plantings and not used all of the same type, you automatically have a built-in method of pest control.

One classic, tragic example of what happens when plant types are not varied is the tale of the Dutch elm disease in America. Spread by a European bark beetle which lives in elms, this fatal disease has ruined the beauty of many streets once lined only with these magnificent trees. The insect was an accidental European import and quickly got out of hand as there was no natural predator here. How easy it was for these beetles to move from one healthy tree to the next up and down the street, leaving barren avenues in their wake.

Varying plant types is similar to the principle of crop rotation used by farmers. And we can follow this literally by varying the places where we plant our annuals each year. It's a good idea, too, to notice which plants seem to attract *or* repel which pests avoiding the reuse of those which attract too many. For example, certain geraniums, chives, and garlic plants appear to repel some aphids and destructive beetles. Marigolds appear to repel certain soil-borne microscopic pests which feed on plant roots. Planting a few of the repelling plants among the others often helps keep the hordes to a tolerable level. This method is commonly referred to as "companion planting."

Ladybug

But, you say, without a background in entomology, how will we know when there is extreme dirty work afoot?

is it a good guy or bad?

In a word, the answer is *observation*. This is the only tool we amateurs have and it is a very useful one at that!

Make a habit of "looking closely at" your plants ("admiring," if you prefer). It is amazing how many remarkable things will be seen. Frequently you can stop problems before they become serious.

a list of some common pests

The following list may help you spot some of the most common pests who might be at work in your garden:

A LIST OF COMMON PESTS

NAME	WHAT TO WATCH FOR	COMMENTS
APHIDS	New growth or leaves near branch ends are deformed or curled. Buds don't open. A sticky honey-like substance is on the leaves.	Aphids are small plant lice with soft pear-shaped bodies and come in assorted colors including green, black, pink, etc. They move slowly in clusters and suck the juice from the buds and new leaves. Woolly aphids are fuzzy or powdery-whitish and prefer the trunk or stems. Appearance may be confused with mealybugs. Aphids may be kept under control with repeated hosings. Interplanting with garlic helps keep them away. Winter spraying of dormant oils is useful for deciduous plants.
BAGWORMS	A 1- or 2-inch long oval-shaped "bag" or bunch of dead leaves or twigs hanging from a branch with numerous chewed or ripped leaves.	Fascinating creatures, bagworms are the larval or worm-like stage of moths. They live and lay their eggs in an oval-shaped bag woven of bits of leaves or twigs. They may be eliminated by snipping off and burning or discarding.
BEETLES	Leaves are chewed-looking, notched, skeletonized, or have a shot-hole appearance.	The thousands of beetle species include many friends. All are recognized by the tough outer case or wing cover which meets in a straight line down the back. Repeated hosings help make them feel unwelcome. (Some beetles do their main damage during their grub or worm-like stage of development.) Winter spraying of dormant oils is useful for deciduous plants.
BORERS	Holes in the trunk or bark, sometimes with piles of sawdust close below.	Borers are the worm-like stage of some beetles or moths. They live within the woody tissues or stems of plants. Cutting away the infested portions or stabbing them with a sharp object poked into their hole helps keep them under control.

A LIST OF COMMON PESTS (continued)

NAME	WHAT TO WATCH FOR	COMMENTS
CATERPILLARS	*Numerous chewed or skeleton-ized leaves or defoliated branches.*	*Caterpillars are the larval or worm-like stage of moths and butterflies and come in an assortment of un-usual colors, shapes, and sizes. Some appear smooth while others have tufts of hairs down their backs. Most blend so perfectly with their surroundings it's hard to see them at first. Manual removal (with or without the aid of a stick) helps keep them under control. Some people may have an allergic reaction (similar to poison ivy) to some of the tufted species.*
LACEBUGS	*Leaves are pale and stippled sort of grayish-looking. Large brown, sticky spots are on the undersides.*	*Lacebugs which attack broadleaved evergreens are a common pest on many terraces. They suck the sap from the underside of the leaves, leaving the plant weakened and dying. The stippled foliage may resemble the effect produced by spider mites, but the large sticky spots which appear on the under-side of the leaf indicate the true nature of the problem. If not extensive, remove badly damaged branches or wipe under-surfaces with a soft brush and soap and water.*
LEAF HOPPERS	*Leaves lose their color and appear to be stippled with numerous white dots.*	*Small insects which hold their wings in a triangular tent-like position, they hop away quickly when disturbed. They feed by sucking the juices from the leaves. Forceful hosings help make them feel unwelcome. Dormant oils useful for control on deciduous plants.*

A LIST OF COMMON PESTS (continued)

NAME	WHAT TO WATCH FOR	COMMENTS
LEAF MINERS	*Leaves have large browned, dead, blotched areas, blisters, or serpentine markings. A hand magnifier discloses a hollow area between leaf surfaces.*	*Leaf miners are the tiny larval or worm-like stage of some flies, beetles, or moths. They live and feed between the leaf surfaces, tunneling or "mining" inside. Difficult to deal with manually if widespread on a large plant such as a birch tree.* *Winter spraying of dormant oils is useful for control.*
LEAF ROLLERS & LEAF TIERS	*Leaves appear rolled or tied neatly into a cigar-like shape.*	*Fascinating caterpillars, these insects live enclosed in a leaf which they have rolled about themselves. Unlike miners, they are on the leaf surface and can be dislodged and destroyed manually or with a strong hosing.*
MEALYBUG	*Sickly-looking foliage and masses of cottony clumps around the joints of the leaves and twigs.*	*Mealybugs are tiny with oval segmented bodies covered with a powdery coating. Typically found in greenhouse and warm weather conditions, they cluster in bunches and suck the plant sap.* *Forceful hosings will keep them under control, but little harm is done to hardy outdoor plants in cold climates, as these insects cannot survive the winter.* *A hand magnifier eliminates possible confusion with woolly aphids which are more fuzzy-looking.*
NEMATODES	*Plant generally lacks vigor, loses leaves, and is stunted or weak.* *Roots are growing poorly and have lesions or tumor-like growths (galls).*	*Nematodes are eel-shaped microscopic animals in the soil. Damage is caused by species that feed on the roots (although a few dine on leaves).* *Certain species of root-feeding nemas are reputed to be repelled by some varieties of marigolds and African daisies.* *Soil disinfectants are available but serious outbreaks may require discarding of all infested soil.*

A LIST OF COMMON PESTS (continued)

NAME	WHAT TO WATCH FOR	COMMENTS
SCALE	Growth is stunted, branches or leaves dying. Small round or oval-shaped bumps (some resembling pimples) on the leaves, needles, or twigs. A sticky honey-like substance may be found on leaf surfaces.	There are numerous small plant-feeding insects called scales. The name describes the armor-like covering developed by most of them in the mature stages. This makes them difficult to deal with at that time. Winter spraying of dormant oils are useful for control on deciduous plants and manual removal is possible if not too widespread.
SPIDER MITES	Foliage is pale and stippled with yellowish or rusty spots. The undersides of the leaves or between the needles may be covered with minute webs.	Mites are very tiny plant-feeders belonging to the class which includes spiders and ticks. They are extremely hard to see until the damage is obvious and their numbers are great. They suck the juices from the leaves and the result looks similar to the work of lacebugs, but the minute cobwebs underscore the difference. A hand magnifier reveals the presence of fast-moving reddish or spotted mites. As the temperature rises, their numbers increase and the fine webs become more apparent. Repeated forceful hosings help keep them under control, and deciduous plants may be sprayed with a dormant oil spray.

A LIST OF COMMON PESTS (continued)

NAME	WHAT TO WATCH FOR	COMMENTS
WEBWORMS and TENT CATERPILLARS	*Masses of silky webs tie together several bunches of leaves, small branch endings, or are interwoven around the crotches of larger branches.*	*Webworms and tent caterpillars are the larval or tiny caterpillar stages of several moths. They make their homes in the finely spun, remarkably strong webs. They feed on the leaves, making the plant both unsightly and weak.* *Strong hosings will dislodge them and help keep them under control, as will pruning away badly infested portions.*
WHITE FLIES	*Clouds of tiny white flies appear suddenly and dart about when the plant is shaken or moved. The leaves are covered with a honey-like substance. Sooty mold often grows on this.*	*Typically found in greenhouse or warm weather conditions, these insects remain quietly sucking the juices from the undersides of leaves during their immature stage. Little long-term damage is incurred by hardy outdoor plants in cold climates, as they cannot survive the cold winter.* *Forceful hosings help wash the eggs away but the cold weather will eliminate them completely. (Carefully wash the undersides of the leaves of houseplants being brought back indoors.)*

A few chewed leaves are a sign of a functioning garden and may be regarded with pride. As discussed before, it is possible to control many pests without wanton overkill.

the last resort
for greedy
hordes

However, some become too greedy, and since the natural predators on terraces are few, the gardener will have to decide whether he has a fair number of free-loaders or is facing a major invasion. If so, it may become necessary for him to deal more firmly with those insects which have gotten out of hand. The important question then is how to use the poisonous weapons at our disposal both wisely and safely.

Chemical insecticides come in an assortment of nasty potentials. Some are safer for mammals than others but they are *all* dangerous and *must* be used with care and respect!

A careless spray can injure a child on the street below as well as poison food plants or pets on the terrace next door. Also, upstairs winds are notoriously unpredictable and if they suddenly reverse you may get it in the face.

read that label

Each year new chemicals appear on the market. Possibly professionals can keep up but the only way amateur gardeners stand a chance is to CAREFULLY READ THE LABEL. By law, that label is required to tell us the true hazard of the material, including which plants may be harmed or damaged by its use. Insecticides considered to be of least danger to man are labeled "CAUTION." The next type is labeled "WARNING" and the most dreadful to be absolutely avoided is labeled "DANGER."

On the label there will also be a list of ingredients (usually terribly complex) with both common and trade names.

Some pesticides must be diluted with water and are to be used only as sprays. Some are in a powder form to be dusted directly on the plant. Others are granular, to be worked full strength into the soil. And finally there are the aerosol cans.

The label will tell you how to use the product properly and woe to the gardener who does not follow the directions to the letter! Incorrect usage (especially excessive amounts) can mean serious injury to the human or to the plant . . . and only the insects may emerge unscathed.

formulations
of pesticides

Despite their convenience I don't like to use the aerosol types. In addition to being relatively expensive, they are easier to handle incorrectly and can do serious damage to the plant. Dusts are useful but may be difficult to handle on windy terraces and tend to make the plants look mildewy.
Where possible I prefer the granular "systemics" which are worked into the soil. When handled carefully and properly (one must wear heavy gloves), this type of pesticide is least likely to fly about and harm the gardener or unsuspecting humans nearby. Also, the principle of the "systemic" action is that the poison is absorbed into the plant and thus only the insect actually eating it will be affected. Systemics give relatively long-lasting protection (some, up to six weeks) and are especially useful for pests like leaf miners which are not easily controlled by surface sprays.
But granular systemics are dangerous and should never be used on plants you intend to eat yourself, such as blueberries, apples, tomatoes, etc. In addition, they do not work on every kind of plant. (You may have to experiment to find out for yourself.) For these plants, as well as all of my edible ones, when all else has failed, I use a liquid or wettable-powder, water-spray mix. If it's the middle of summer and I'm convinced that the plant

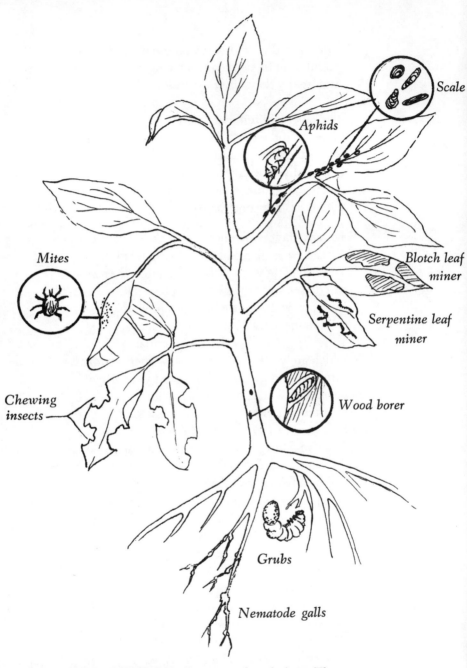

Scale

Aphids

Mites

Blotch leaf miner

Serpentine leaf miner

Chewing insects

Wood borer

Grubs

Nematode galls

SOME INSECT PROBLEMS—(Drawing adapted from The New York State College of Agriculture at Cornell University Cooperative Extension Bulletin)

won't survive another minute, I spray immediately. However, most of the time, it is possible to wait a while. In such cases I delay treatment until the following fall or spring and apply what is known as a "dormant" spray.

dormant sprays

Dormant sprays, as the name implies, are used on deciduous plants after they have lost their leaves and are in their dormant period. They are used on a day when the temperature is expected to remain well above freezing, either in late fall or very early spring (before there is any color showing on the buds).

They need be applied only once and will kill overwintering insect eggs as well as many disease-producing organisms. Because there are no leaves on the plant, there are fewer surfaces to spray and so it's a fairly simple matter. Because they are used during the cold weather, they are less likely to injure birds or other beneficial predators.

Some of the common products presently available for home garden use are as follows:

A LIST OF PESTICIDES

(The following products are presented as examples only. This list is not all-inclusive and is not to be considered an endorsement of any one company or product.)

TRADE NAMES	PRODUCT GENERALLY USEFUL FOR	COMMENTS	GENERIC NAME
MALATHION 50 (spray) CYTHION® (same but less odor)	*many pests including aphids, mealybugs, white flies, mites, some scale insects, thrips, lacebugs*	*Used for a wide range of chewing and sucking pests, these may also be applied to edible plants. Should not be used when temperatures are expected to exceed about 85°F. May injure some plants including ferns, lantana, viburnum, jade, maples, white pine, sweetpeas. Consider toxic to fish and bees, but relatively short-lasting.*	*malathion*
SEVIN® (spray)	*many pests including caterpillars, beetles, slugs, snails, web-worms, leaf miners, some soil insects*	*Used for a wide range of chewing insects, this spray may also be applied to edible plants. May injure tender foliage, especially during periods of high humidity. Not to be used on Boston ivies, Virginia creeper, and possibly harmful to coton-easter. May cause buildup of spider mites. Very toxic to honey bees.*	*carbaryl*

A LIST OF PESTICIDES (continued)

TRADE NAMES	PRODUCT GENERALLY USEFUL FOR	COMMENTS	GENERIC NAME
DORMANT OIL (dormant spray) VOLCK® OIL SPRAY ("summer" spray)	many pests including scale insects, mealybugs, mites, aphids, overwintering eggs of many summer problems (dormant oils only)	Dormant oils and summer oils often are the same product in different dilutions for use during the respective seasons. Dormant oil sprays are sometimes combined with fungicides to eliminate overwintering pathogens. They are applied when the deciduous plants have lost their leaves and may be used anytime the temperature is not less than 45°F. (late fall, early spring or both). Summer strength sprays may be used when plants are in full leaf. Some oil sprays may be injurious when used on evergreens and thin barked trees such as maple or beech.	petroleum oils
KELTHANE® (spray) TEDION (spray)	mites	Considered safe for use on edible plants, these products may harm lantanas, nasturtiums, cyclamens, and tender new growth. Toxic to fish.	dicofol tetradifon
ISOTOX® (systemic spray and soil granules) SCIENCE SYSTEMIC (systemic spray) BONIDE (systemic spray and soil granules) CYGON® (systemic spray)	many insects including leaf miners, scale, mites, thrips, white flies	Systemic action sprays or soil granules enter into the system of the plant and provide a relatively long-lasting poisonous effect. They are never to be used for edible plants, and must always be handled with extreme caution. Soil granules are useful in minimizing wind-spray accidents and harm to helpful insects. Toxic to fish and wildlife.	di-syston

A LIST OF PESTICIDES (continued)

TRADE NAMES	PRODUCT GENERALLY USEFUL FOR	COMMENTS	GENERIC NAME
Botanicals (sprays) (aerosols)	*many insects*	*Insecticides derived from plant sources are available in several forms, often in combination with other ingredients. Considered safe for edible plants, they are as poisonous as some synthetics and should be accorded equal respect. Toxic to fish.*	*rotenone* *pyrethrum*
SPECTRACIDE® (spray)	*many insects including aphids, scale, leaf miners, white flies, spider mites, some soil insects*	*Used for a wide range of sucking insects and some soil pests, this spray may injure some plants including gardenia, hibiscus, poinsettia.*	*diazinon*
BORER-KIL (paste)	*borers*	*Borers may be difficult to deal with. Sprays aid in preventing penetration of insect into plant. Once inside, injection of toxic pastes directly into hole is probably most efficient method.*	*lindane*
V.C. 13® *NEMAGON®* *FUMAZONE®*	*some nematodes and soil insects*	*Flooding of soil in containers is often difficult, dangerous, and futile. Nematodes may be inside roots. If problem is very widespread, either leave entire area unplanted for several years, or discard infested soil completely, scrub planter and begin again.*	

There are many spray-type applicators available. If your garden is small or you have no tall trees, it's easy to use a hand-squeezable quart-size plastic bottle which can be found in hardware stores. But be sure to look for those with adjustable nozzles that permit both a fine mist and a long stream. On my terrace, the trees are now quite high, so I also have what is known as a "trombone" sprayer. This instrument utilizes an arm-swing rather than a hand-squeeze, to build up the pressure and it will throw spray as far as 15 feet or so. I never use the siphon type of "hose end" sprayer. Water pressure in my apartment building can vary widely from one minute to the next and I don't trust it to dilute the product properly.

sprayer equipment

In any case, treat *only* the plant under attack, spraying just to the point of "runoff." Be sure to keep all poisonous products and accompanying equipment *out of your kitchen*. Use a separate set of measuring spoons, funnel, or mixing dishes. No matter how well you may think you are cleaning them, it is not worth the price you may pay if you use a kitchen spoon which you then return to the cabinet.

Also, whenever possible, do the mixing outside (a good place to work is right on the floor). The bathroom sink can be your second choice but the kitchen sink, never!

When dealing with pesticides, I am guided by the warnings issued to commercial nurserymen from the College of Agriculture at Cornell. These include the following:

safety first

1. Wear protective clothing such as gloves, long sleeves, slacks, hair cover, etc.
2. Wash hands and face carefully afterwards and change all clothes, including undergarments.

3. Never eat, smoke, or chew while preparing or applying pesticides.
4. Store the products in their original containers in a safe cabinet out of reach of children or pets.
5. If any symptoms of illness occur during or shortly after application, call a physician immediately.

disposal of
unused
pesticides

A tricky problem facing users of pesticides is "what to do with what's left over." These products lose their effectiveness when stored in diluted form and anyway are too dangerous to have sitting around a small apartment. It's useful to try to mix only enough for one spraying or use up all that you have mixed. But sometimes I find I do have more than I or my neighbors can use and then I'm stuck.

It is *very* poor practice to pour these things straight down a sink, toilet, or floor drain. Yard gardeners are often advised to sprinkle what's left over, around a little-used portion of their garden. This is supposed to help filter it through the soil before it reaches the nearest water supply. I try to imitate this method by diluting it with water first, and then pouring it onto "little-used" portions of several of my largest containers.

And that's the best I can come up with.

Aphids

The first step in dealing with pests is figuring out what is really happening so that you can then figure out how to deal with them. This is true of other plant problems as well.

nonpathogenic troubles

As Dr. Jerry Walker, pathologist, formerly with the Brooklyn Botanic Garden, taught his classes there, a number of *environmental* problems may cause symptoms which are similar to more serious ones. Although relatively simple in cause, nonpathogenic troubles often plague beginners and can abruptly end a glorious gardening career.

The most widespread of these is incorrect watering. Watering is so important I have devoted all of Section 6 to it alone. (I have no scientific statistics, but I strongly suspect improper watering to be *the* major cause of plant death on balconies and terraces.) The next main nonpathogenic problem is the incorrect or overenthusiastic use of fertilizers, pesticides, or both. (Read that label!)

Insufficient light (which really is having the wrong plant for the particular environmental conditions) ranks next for the dubious honor of prime discourager of amateurs.

And the last major nonpathogenic headache is plant malnutrition. This is the result of nutrient deficiencies in the soil or an incorrect acidity or pH soil value for the plant in question. (See Section 10.)

spotting problems early

But, you say, without proper training how do you know when you have a problem? Well, without a degree in medicine, how does a conscientious parent know when his or her child is getting sick so that the doctor may be called? Again, the answer is *observation*. If you make a habit of looking at your plants, you will know what they are like when they are healthy and happy. Thus you will quickly recognize when they are not.

A flowering shrub which is normally stiff, with

upright branches and lustrous green leaves, is
telling you something is wrong when it begins to
droop, no longer flowers, or the leaves lose their
healthy appearance. As I said before, if you look,
you will be surprised at what you see . . . and that
includes the early stages of many problems,
nonpathogenic and otherwise.

For plants are living things.

And they do get sick sometimes (just like people,
dogs, and tropical fish). Often they can be helped
if the cause is determined early.

plants get sick like people

The main causal factors in plant sicknesses are
bacteria, fungi, viruses, and nematodes (microscopic
animals). Sometimes the symptoms are similar and
only diagnosis by a plant pathologist can pinpoint
the true nature of the cause. However, general
medicines in the form of sprays are available which
help control a wide variety of these problems.
Unfortunately, certain virus-caused diseases* are
difficult to deal with and the only alternative may
be to get rid of the plant.

But, in any case, it is especially helpful to make use
of basic sanitation and antiseptic practices. This
includes removing fallen diseased leaves and as
much of the obviously afflicted limbs and twigs as
possible. And when dealing with sick plants, as
Cynthia Westcott says, the gardener should try to
be like "a surgeon going from one patient to
another": clean hands and clean instruments. The
gardener may succeed in transferring the problem
far better than any parasite. A strong household
disinfectant, such as Clorox, helps "sterilize"
garden tools. The following list may help in dealing
with some of the problems most often encountered.

* Dr. Walker informs me that another group called "myco-
plasmas" is now also believed to cause serious diseases for
which no cure has yet been found.

LIST OF COMMON AILMENTS AND SOME FIRST AID

SYMPTOM (and typical "name")	PROBLEM MAY BE	POSSIBLE TREATMENT
edges or tips of leaves are burned (SCORCH)	too little water reaching ends	increase frequency and/or quantity of water
		lighten soil mixture to permit easy penetration of water
	too strong direct sun and/or wind for plant variety	shield or move plant to less sunny and/or windy spot
	overfeeding with chemical fertilizers	flood soil with water to wash away excess
		read label carefully before applying
	potash deficiency	have soil analyzed and use potash-high fertilizer
spots or holes on leaves resembling polka dots (LEAF SPOT)	beetles or other insects	refer to list of pests
	a variety of bacterial or fungus diseases often worsened by wet weather conditions	IGNORE if not widespread but sanitation important, remove and destroy fallen leaves or very infected portions, use dormant sprays for overwintering spores
		SPRAY WITH sprays containing Zineb, Ferbam, Maneb, Captan, or Benomyl
		seek professional help if persistent in subsequent years
whitish coating on leaves (POWDERY MILDEW)	fungus growth often resulting from wet conditions	IGNORE if not widespread but refrain from wetting leaves especially in evenings or during periods of high humidity and no wind
		remove badly infected leaves, prune for increased circulation
		SPRAY WITH sprays containing Folpet or Benomyl

LIST OF COMMON AILMENTS AND SOME FIRST AID (continued)

SYMPTOM (and typical "name")	PROBLEM MAY BE	POSSIBLE TREATMENT
entire branch endings and leaves blackened (FIRE BLIGHT)	a variety of bacterial diseases	remove all afflicted portions, pruning well back below blighted area (disinfect tools) if persistent and recurring seek professional help
leaves die and fall	improper watering	check soil carefully for moisture to correct watering procedures
	problem at root level (disease or parasite)	check roots for obvious signs of abnormality (rot, lumps, parasites, etc.) seek professional help
leaves blotched and browned on wide areas	sun or wind burn	move or shield from strong sun or wind increase water
	(check with hand magnifier for leaf miners)	(refer to list of pests and pesticides)
	several possible fungus diseases	IGNORE if not widespread but sanitation important, remove all infested portions and fallen leaves use dormant sprays to destroy overwintering spores SPRAY WITH sprays containing Ferbam, Maneb, Zineb, Benomyl if persistent in subsequent years seek professional help
	air pollutants	join and help the work of conservation organizations

LIST OF COMMON AILMENTS AND SOME FIRST AID (continued)

SYMPTOM (and typical "name")	PROBLEM MAY BE	POSSIBLE TREATMENT
lumps, swellings, or roundish growths on twigs, trunks, leaves, or roots (GALLS)	local swellings of plant tissues	IGNORE if on upper part of plant, not widespread, and plant is not appearing to suffer
	insects or miscellaneous diseases	check for presence of insects
		if at the root level and/or plant is appearing to weaken seek professional help
	(do not confuse with "scale")	see list of pests
leaves droop, branch endings are limp (WILT)	too little water reaching ends	increase frequency and/or quantity of water
		lighten soil mixture for easier penetration of moisture
	a variety of fungus diseases	remove afflicted portions and destroy (disinfect tools)
	root problem (disease or parasite)	check for signs of abnormality (rot, lumps, insects)
		if persistent and widespread seek professional help
sooty or sticky substance on leaves	"honey dew" produced by many insects	(see list of pests)
	mold or mildew growing in "honey dew" secretion	remove leaves if not widespread and keep pests under control
vertical cracks on trunk or large limbs (WINTER INJURY)	cold dry weather causes cracking of bark in exposed sunny locations	wrap trunks of young trees or shrubs
		avoid late summer feedings
		mulch well and check for water need during winter

LIST OF COMMON AILMENTS AND SOME FIRST AID (continued)

SYMPTOM (and typical "name")	PROBLEM MAY BE	POSSIBLE TREATMENT
leaves paling or yellowing, especially between veins (CHLOROSIS)	mineral deficiency (usually nitrogen)	work fresh organic matter into soil
		feed with nitrogen-high fertilizer
	lack of available iron because of incorrect pH (especially on evergreens)	get leaf and/or soil analysis to determine proper pH value for plant species
	trace elements missing	
	insufficient oxygen around roots	lighten soil to prevent waterlogging
general poor health, some leaf loss or discolorations	malnutrition	work fresh organic matter into soil
		feed with general fertilizer
		if persistent have leaves and/or soil analyzed for missing nutrients
		IGNORE if occurring in the fall but rework soil when leaves drop
new leaves small, of poor quality, dis-colored, misshapen, or mottled	malnutrition	work fresh organic matter into soil
		feed with general fertilizer
		have leaves analyzed for missing nutrients
	insufficient light	move to better light conditions
	viruses	remove and destroy
		seek professional help if persistent and widespread
no flowers	malnutrition	work fresh organic matter into soil
	phosphorus deficiency	feed with phosphorus-high fertilizers
	(if accompanied by good leaf growth)	discontinue feeding with fertilizer high in nitrogen
	improper photo period	move to greater light conditions
twig dieback	root damage, from excessive water	prune back to healthy portion, improve drainage by lightening soil
	(if after dormancy) insufficient water	IGNORE, but remember to check for moisture need during next dormant period

Studying this section (or even several whole books) will not enable you to cure or even recognize all plant problems any more than learning first aid will mean you are a doctor. So when a valuable plant is in serious trouble, by all means turn to the professionals (Appendix 2).

Sometimes, an accurate verbal description of the symptoms will suffice. But generally it is better to submit samples of the plant for diagnosis.

Follow the cutting, packing, and information procedures used for plant identification (see page 16) and write a concise history of your observations, including:

1. how long you have been aware of the symptoms
2. the extent of the problem over the different plant parts
3. whether any other terrace plants manifest similar symptoms
4. normal recent feeding and/or watering procedures
5. recent general weather conditions in the area
6. anything else you think may be helpful

Paraphrasing my grandmother's statement regarding children . . . "little plants little problems, big plants big problems." This is not to say that the size of the plant necessarily minimizes the problem. But certainly in the case of a young specimen of a common species it makes things a lot easier. We are not dealing with venerable hundred-year-old oaks. For this reason the best cure for a terrace plant which is *persistently* troubled by disease or insects is . . . the garbage pail!

We have neither the time nor space to spare for constant problems and must be ruthless about them

Marginal notes:

seeking professional help

persistently troublesome plants

when the time comes. It is pure masochism to submit to continued aggravation when a healthy replacement might appreciate your loving home more.

Once the decision to discard the old and start anew has been reached, the sick plant should be dug out carefully and placed immediately in a large bag for disposal. It is a good idea also to remove a substantial portion of the surrounding soil which has been in direct contact with the plant.
You may assume mostly that the problem is confined to the upper portions.
And often enough this is the case.
But, as Dr. Walker pointedly told his classes in Brooklyn, you must study the entire plant when there is a problem . . . and this includes the *roots*.
For plantings confined to the limited soil in containers, this is vital!
Thus, upon removing any plant, remember always to look closely at the roots as well as surrounding subsurface soil. If you ever repotted a houseplant

checking the
roots

you will have a general sense of what healthy roots look like: white and full with numerous fine terminal hairs. Healthy roots have no mushy sections, rot, mold, or unusual lumpy growths. (Members of the Pea or Legume family have tubercles or lumps known as "nodules" on their roots which are normal and not indicative of a malaise. A few nonleguminous plants, including Russian olive, do too.)
If you feel there is something unusual about the way the sick plant's roots look and do not know what it is or why, check into the matter further with the help of a professional before replanting that area.

For two years I struggled to maintain life in a lovely

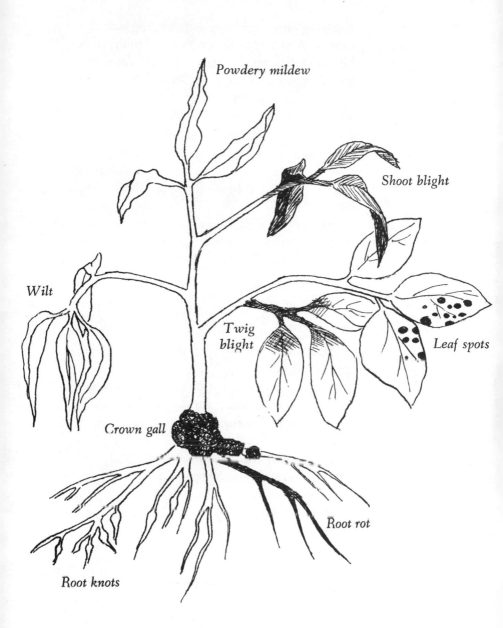

Powdery mildew

Shoot blight

Wilt

Twig
blight

Leaf spots

Crown gall

Root rot

Root knots

SOME PLANT DISEASES—(Drawing adapted from The
New York State College of Agriculture at Cornell University
Cooperative Extension Bulletin)

flowering plum tree, with a depressing lack of success. When I finally gave up and pulled it out, I discovered to my horror there were tumor-like growths completely covering its roots. My worst fears were then confirmed by Dr. Pascal Pirone at The New York Botanical Garden; a bacterial disease-causing organism was *in the soil*.

soil disposal

So in addition to discarding the sick plant, in some cases it may be necessary to discard an enormous amount of surrounding soil and possibly the entire tub.

Unlike your yard gardening counterparts, you must do your planting over and over again in precisely the same spot. This means that if there is a serious problem which originates in the soil, it is likely that this area is harboring and will continue to harbor microscopic causes of the trouble. A new plant placed in that same soil could easily become the next victim, especially if it is the same or a closely related species.

Although soil fumigants are available there may be no practical way, really, for the small terrace gardener to deal with infected soil, except by disposal.

workmen who
tear up the
garden

You do not qualify as a bona fide terrace gardener until you have survived the havoc wreaked by at least one set of building workmen. Ranking with destructive insects and diseases, this is a problem which sooner or later confronts many terrace owners especially in high-rise structures. Workmen may come to paint, repair leaks (real or imagined), or fix the roofing or parapet walls. They generally arrive in the spring just as the buds stir and break, to do a little stirring and breaking themselves. There is not much advice I can offer on the subject . . . other than to grin and bear it and hope when

they leave that the work *was* needed and
necessary.

On a number of occasions when workmen came to
attack "leaks" on my terrace, my "garden" was not
the culprit after all.* In my apartment building (as
in others with "setbacks") there are pipes below the
terrace floor, hung from the ceiling of the
apartment beneath which cause many of the wet
conditions they blame on terraces. Sometimes, too,
the metal flashing or waterproofing in the wall is
damaged—again, no fault of the plants.

protect or
move your
plants

When workmen must work outside, however, it is
a real advantage to have plants in containers which
may be moved to a safe place. If not, try to stall the
workers until a professional gardener can dig up
and wrap the plants' roots properly for removal.
This is done most safely when the plants are in a
dormant state. A free (?) root pruning may be your
only consolation for the devastation . . . but, rest
assured, this is a universal problem in upstairs
gardens.

As with humans, then, one may expect a few
(health) problems. But, as with humans, a little
early observation and diagnosis frequently results in
the plant's recovering and living on to a ripe old age.
And if the *weather* is good, raising plants on a
balcony, terrace, rooftop, penthouse, or patio can
be lovely.

---

* Be prepared to be blamed for any and all building problems near or not so near your terrace. Perhaps because of
their visibility, your plants will be accused continually.

A CLUSTER OF
WOOLLY
APHIDS ON A
CRAB-APPLE
TREE

A ROSEBUD
BECOMES FOOD
FOR APHIDS

THE DARK
BROWN SHELLS
OF MATURE
SCALE INSECTS
FEASTING ON
A BRANCH

A BRANCH OF
CLIMBING
EUONYMUS
COVERED WITH
WHITE SCALE

SKELETONIZED
AND MISSING
LEAVES EATEN
BY A
CATERPILLAR

OUR FRIEND,
THE LADYBUG

WHEN
WORKMEN ARE
AROUND,
PROTECT YOUR
PLANTS AS
BEST YOU CAN

CHERRY TREE LEAVES WITH THE "SHOT HOLE" APPEARANCE WHICH RESULTS FROM A BACTERIAL DISEASE

A TWIG OF PIERIS JAPONICA WITH THE FOLIAGE MOTTLED BY ANDROMEDA LACEBUG; THE UNDER SURFACE IS COVERED WITH DARK STICKY SPOTS

Holly berries

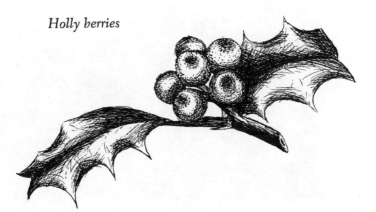

Frost! You may fall!
After chrysanthemums there are
no flowers at all!

Ōemaru

Section 8

Important Tasks for Fall

As the warmth of summer fades into the chill of fall,
the inevitability of winter is apparent in the form of
several dank and dreary days.

a fall mood   At this time, a peculiar mood sets in . . .
It starts slowly and inconspicuously, but it comes
upon the terrace gardener most surely. It is the
"end-of-summer-gardening" blues. This is not a
mourning of the summer's end. On the contrary, it
is a desire for the dormant season to begin. A
longing for a period in which we humans too may
have a chance to rest.
Flowers are allowed to go to seed where previously
"dead heads" were meticulously removed . . .
trees and shrubs are no longer watched over with
the care of before . . . the sweeping and hosing,
joyous chores of sunny summer mornings, all now
regarded as drudgery.
Daily, the garden seems a little less than perfect
but the erstwhile devoted gardener looks the other
way. Colorful annuals begin to fade. They become
spindly and yellowed and go to seed while the trees
drop their leaves all over the floor.
Furnaces throughout town, increasing their efforts
in preparation of the cold, emit more soot than
ever. Fall marks the beginning of new civic
involvements and seasonal household chores

demand time formerly devoted to the terrace. The sun seems to race to the horizon and early darkness overtakes outdoor tasks previously completed after dinner.

I'm ashamed to admit it, but every fall I wonder if I have completely lost interest in my precious oasis in the sky.
I begin to wonder, is it all worth the effort . . . trees and shrubs and flowers maintained in containers. The watering, feeding, constant alert for parasites and disease . . . I know I have lost my fight to at least one invader and new summer roots consume more water than before. It is time to begin taking in the houseplants, but the task looms monumentally before me. I think, "God, I hope spring never comes." I know it's too early to take in the plastic hose . . . but I want to go dormant too . . .
This is fall. And I have come to accept this as a fall mood.

Marigold

an objective look

This period, then, is the time to stand back and objectively look at your little garden since you may as well take advantage of this emotion. Feelings about plants are remarkably similar to those one has for humans. There are some you care for greatly but there are also ones you now don't like at all. With the memory of summer's beauty, as well as its chores, still fresh, you may perceive these feelings more readily. A rational reason for liking or disliking a particular specimen may not even be possible.

plants you're unhappy with

If you find yourself unhappy with a plant, don't agonize, just get rid of it! As a tiny garden owner you do not have the time or space to devote to plants which have proven to be unfortunate selections, whatever the reason.

In the case of a small or inexpensive shrub or tree, just pull it out and throw it away. If it is unyielding or the roots are too entwined with other plants in the container, cut it down and wait until spring to remove the stump.

I once had a climber rose which was so thorny it was a menace to anyone who came near it. To make matters worse, two summers came and went and not one bloom appeared. Much as I adore my other roses, I was genuinely relieved when I threw this one away.

plants unhappy with you

There are also times when a potentially attractive plant is obviously not happy with *you*. And this, too, is cause for getting rid of it. There are very few plants which, if purchased at a reputable local nursery, will not *survive* demanding conditions. But, for one reason or another, it is possible they have not done as well as one would have wanted.

In cases where a large or expensive specimen is involved, it's difficult just to discard it. Sometimes a friend with a different terrace condition or a country garden (and car) might be interested in a living gift.

giving plants away

In the absence of such a friend, you can investigate donating it to a school or park. Since you will probably foot the bill for transporting and replanting (this could be expensive), consider such a donation only where a valuable tree or shrub is involved. An accountant might advise on a possible tax deduction for such a "gift."

It is best to avoid giving trees or shrubs which will remain in containers unless there is substantial evidence that the recipient is capable of maintaining them. Institutions such as schools and churches are rarely equipped to cope with them and so the plant's best chance for survival after leaving your terrace is to be replanted in the ground.
In any case, don't feel guilty about being ruthless and getting rid of plants which have not worked out and this is definitely the easiest time of the year to do it!
Throw it away, or give it away, but spend your precious gardening time enjoying every inch of the terrace.

While our country cousin is furiously raking leaves from the lawn, so we terrace gardeners must observe our own variation of this fall ritual . . . with a broom.

fall cleanup Moist rotting leaves collect behind and between (and under) the containers as well as in the drains. They provide a perfect haven for summer's unwanted pests to begin a new life cycle (both the multilegged creatures as well as a myriad of microscopic organisms less easily observed).
A broom plus a dustpan plus a trip to the trash pail is the formula for preventing many of next summer's problems.
This is also the time to pull out dead or dying annuals. There is nothing so depressing on a fall terrace as the wizened remains of a colorful summer past.

Bagworm on evergreen

life without a
compost pile

Having to discard dead terrace leaves or plants in the fall is most distressing to those who would like to maintain a compost pile from which to derive fertile humus for the garden. The late organic gardening specialist J. I. Rodale frequently noted the importance of compost, in his writings.

It is a real shame to throw away this potentially valuable matter, but it is often more prudent for the owner of a small terrace to do so.

Usually several seasons are needed to produce the right degree of decomposition as well as a compost free of disease-producing organisms or insect pests. So, rare are those apartment dwellers who can maintain a year-round pile themselves.

But this is not to say that small compost piles cannot or do not exist, even in mid-Manhattan. For if maintained properly, they neither smell nor are visually offensive to the serious gardener.

but if there's
room to
spare . . .

One terrace compost pile I saw recently was contained in a slatted wood box, roughly 3 feet in each direction. It was raised several inches off the floor, had a hinged cover, and was painted an unobtrusive color. Well-rotted vegetable matter

from the owner's kitchen was added, along with
the discards from the garden. To aid the microbes
already at work, a commercial product was used
periodically. There are several on the market, but
this one was the "Quick Compost Maker" from the
Farm Equipment Co., Wintersville, Ohio. I admit
to having been most envious of the rich humus
this city dweller had at his disposal, all year long.
(In fact, I became so inspired, I immediately
started searching my terrace for a spot where I
could do likewise.)

Although composting can take many months, the
process can be accelerated considerably if the matter
used is chopped up fine before being thrown on the
pile. To do this, some suburban gardeners use
shredding machines. But one New York City
penthouse gardener, Stewart Mott, felt that
compost was so essential to his garden, he decided
to get a small shredder too. Quantities of vegetables,
herbs, and fruit grown in his large garden high
above Manhattan are frequently distributed to both
his household and office staffs.

Mr. Mott, who is known less for his gardening than
for his civic activities, noted that groups of
individual, small terrace owners might well work
together and use a communal area, such as the roof
of their apartment building, for a "community
compost" heap. In so doing, they would not only be
creating a more fertile soil for their own gardens,
but would be taking another step toward the
proper recycling of organic household wastes.
(Which some forward-looking communities are
already attempting to do, on a municipal level.)

Even though the awning is shut up tight and the
chairs covered for storing, it is still too soon to put
away all the tools. The first brisk autumn day may

smaller pieces
compost faster

"community
composting"

make its appearance but vital life processes continue.

"dormant"
means sleep

The plants have had a busy summer, during which they have grown new roots and utilized the available nutrients in their containers. The continual leaching from these planters is a fact of life and additionally reduces the food supply. Furthermore, by summer's end the soil may have become quite compact.

But "dormant" means *sleep*.

It is similar to the hibernation of animals during which there are *slowed* life processes, not NO life processes. Small quantities of both nutrients and water (see Section 6) will be required by the plants' systems all winter long. Thus when most of the leaves have dropped it is time to loosen the soil (adding perlite if necessary) as well as work in some fresh matter.

fall cultivation

You may start this fall cultivation of the tubs by using a narrow hand trowel or fork and digging in along the outer portion of the containers turning the soil up and over. Work around the edges and then back to within about 8 inches or so of the trunk.

Don't get nervous if you find that you have cut a few roots here and there. This minimal amount of "root pruning" will not harm the plant and is actually beneficial for our restricted container residents. By turning the soil over this way you will be aerating and loosening it as well as exposing pesty subsoil insect eggs to the winter elements.

Since at this time of the year we do not wish to encourage new plant growth (it can't develop sufficiently to withstand the winter and even in warm climates the plants need a chance to rest), the nutrients we add must be only slow-acting ones. As it is also important to restore the humus-making property to our soil, natural organic and mineral substances, rather than chemical fertilizers, should be used. (This subject is discussed in detail later in Section 10.) If you have any friends in the country, let them supply you with "humus producers" in the form of well-rotted compost or leaf mold. Otherwise, buy bags of dehydrated cow manure at the nearest garden center.

spring begins
in the fall

As you dig in and turn over the soil, mix in a very generous handful of whatever you have gotten for every 2 feet or so of plant height. If necessary, remove some of the old soil to make room.

It has been said that good gardeners know that "spring begins in the fall." So now you can also restore nutrients which promote good bloom among early flowering plants. To do this for your deciduous trees and shrubs like crab apples, forsythia, cherries, etc. add in a handful of *bone meal* for each 4 feet or so of height. For the broadleaved evergreens like rhododendron, azalea, pieris japonica, etc. use half the amount of bone meal or substitute superphosphate, along with some peat moss.

And, of course, now is the time to plant those spring-flowering tulips and crocuses you wished you had had last year.

Gardening books abound with a variety of elaborate procedures to protect plants from the winter. This includes burlap, wood buffers, and "hilling up" the soil around stems.

winter
"protection"

My feeling is that if the varieties I have selected can't make it on their own through the New York winter, then they don't belong on my terrace. I want to look at my *plants* in the snow and refuse to clutter up the scene with piles of burlap or other eyesores.

Some gardeners advocate using an "antidesiccant"

Spruce cone

spray to help prevent winter dehydration. But after hearing most of the pros and cons, I've decided it's a waste of my time and money and I don't bother with it.

So aside from making sure all the climbers are secure and not flapping in the wind, there is very little I believe in doing for "protection" from the winter.

adding evergreen boughs

After the first real freeze, an additional mulch of bark, which won't blow away, may be added onto the tubs. This helps stabilize the soil temperature and retain moisture. Later on, it's nice to cut up holiday evergreens and spread the boughs around. Although the dropped needles eventually add to the nutrients in the containers, more than anything else I regard these boughs as winter "consolation," as well as a useful way to end a Christmas tree's life. Finally, after checking the wild bird feeders to make sure they are well stocked, for the moment at least, it's time to sit back and enjoy at last the beginning of your own period of dormancy.

LEAVES
FALL FROM
THE
SOURWOOD
TREE AND
THE IMPATIENS
FLOWERS.
BELOW. THE
WEEPING ELM
IN THE
FOREGROUND
(LEFT) IS
NEARLY BARE

ORANGE FALL
BERRIES ON A
MOUNTAIN
ASH

**FUTURE
GENERATIONS
OF SOME OF
SUMMER'S
PESTS MAY
EASILY BE
PREVENTED**

CLEAR OUT
FLOOR DRAINS

REMOVE DEAD
ANNUALS

THE CATKINS
ON THE BIRCH
PROVIDE AN
INTERESTING
LATE FALL
SILHOUETTE.
THE PRIVET AT
THE RIGHT
KEEPS ITS
LEAVES
LONGER

SMALL CRAB
APPLES MAY
REMAIN INTO
EARLY WINTER
FOR ANOTHER
UNIQUE
OUTLINE

REMEMBER, SPRING BEGINS IN THE FALL WHEN CROCUS OR TULIP BULBS ARE PLANTED IN THE TREE TUB

STORE-BOUGHT EVERGREEN BOUGHS SUPPLEMENT THOSE ALREADY GROWING ON THIS TERRACE. IN THE SPRING, THE DROPPED NEEDLES CAN BE WORKED INTO THE SOIL

Of what use are twigs
but to sweep up a litter
of fallen petals?
Buson

Section 9

Some Pruning Basics

While reading an old English gardening book, I was
startled by the author's simile that pruning was like
a surgical operation in being a "necessary evil."
This negative attitude toward one of the most
creative and important aspects of gardening is just
not understandable.
It's true that pruning is cutting away portions of a
plant.
But the gloomy similarity ends there.
Suffice it to say that I prefer to be influenced by the
positive attitudes and artistic achievements of
learning from   Japanese bonsai gardeners and I hope you will be
bonsai   too. Translated from the Japanese, bonsai means
"tray planting." But for our purposes it may be
interpreted as "keeping mature plants growing
happily in a limited area."
And proper pruning enables us to do just that.

For the terrace gardener, there is much to be gained
from studying bonsai techniques and nowhere is
this more evident than in the area of pruning,
both *above* the ground as well as *below* (more
about below in Section 10). I have no intention of
maintaining a 200-year-old pine in a 4-inch pot on
my terrace. However, the very existence of such a
specimen in the Brooklyn Botanic Garden's bonsai

collection makes me feel less defensive about maintaining my 12-foot birch tree in a 3-foot tub. (This, by the way, is one answer to cynical people who question the health and well-being of terrace trees and shrubs in containers.)

Putting the nuances of pruning aesthetics aside for a moment, what are some of the primary reasons for cutting away portions of a plant?

the "3 d's" of pruning: dead, damaged, diseased

Beginning with what may be called the first of the "3 D's," the basic reason for pruning is to remove dead wood. A particularly awful winter, for example, may mean the death of some branches or parts of branches. This becomes evident when they do not "leaf out" in the spring even though the rest of the plant has already done so. The extent of the dead portion can be found by noting the point where live buds are actually beginning to stir. Or, in the case of a plant which is in full leaf in midsummer, the point where the first set of healthy leaves or branches occurs. All pruning is done pretty much the same way: the cut is made just *above* this first sign of life, as close to it as possible, and at an angle, as shown in the illustration.

a good cut is a clean cut

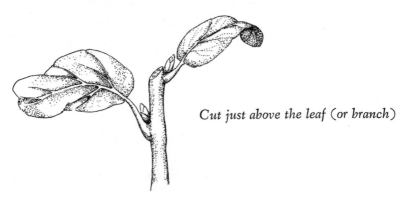

Cut just above the leaf (or branch)

Getting rid of dead wood may involve removing large branches, but it can also mean removing a few inches. Thus, using your fingernail to nip off a dead geranium leaf may also be included in this category.

The logical extension of this, the second of the "3 D's," is the cutting away of any broken or severely damaged branches. It doesn't matter if these resulted from a bad storm or a difficult elevator ride. The principle is the same.

And the third "D" is the removal of areas which are diseased or parasite-infested. For example, the tiny bothersome insects known as aphids like to cluster on the tips of the plant they are attacking. Instead of a mad dash to the poison shelf, often it is just as effective for the gardener to pinch off the afflicted inch or two.

The removal of diseased portions occasionally includes something as drastic as discarding the *entire plant*. And this is not to be discounted as another extremely effective form of "pruning."

Crowded conditions are no better for plants than for people. After a period of rapid growth, some shrubs and trees become too dense for their own health and provide us with the next reason for pruning. When leaves and branches overlap to the point of reducing air circulation and preventing the penetration of light, pruning is necessary to correct the situation.

opening to
light and air

Aside from looking like a hopelessly tangled mess, an overgrown plant will begin to lose its inner leaves and a spindly appearance results. Parasites or disease may take over the crowded interior branches and the plant's ability to flower may also be reduced.

Quite often it is possible to prevent excessive denseness before it starts. This is done by removing new or young branches whose growth pattern is unmistakably in and toward the center of the plant itself. Get them while they're young, since cutting off older branches is a lot harder.

directional pruning

Look at your plant carefully. The position and location of every bud actually tells you where that branch is going to go. By cutting back to just ABOVE a bud which is *pointing toward* a more desirable direction, it is possible to redirect the future growth of the plant. This method of predicting and then affecting the future is known as "directional pruning" and its application on a terrace is limitless.

Many bushy plants such as forsythia or deutzia produce their flowers on young wood. Thus an older shrub which is quite overgrown may lose its vigor as well as its ability to bloom. In order to keep

rejuvenation of old shrubs

the flowering potential at a peak, it's necessary to remove some of the mature growth.

First-time pruning of overgrown older shrubs follows a "rule-of-thumb" which permits a to-the-soil-line removal of as much as one-third of all old branches in one year. New young shoots, known as "suckers," will then grow from the base and result in a rejuvenation of the plant.

creating "trees" from shrubs

On the other hand, by using the reverse procedure and eliminating this new growth, nurserymen can create a "tree" out of a normally shrubby plant. These "trees" are known as "standards," and you may see such specimens in catalogues, the most typical being the "rose-tree" or the "geranium-tree." But it is also possible for you to use this method on a larger scale and encourage greater height of otherwise bushy plants. Such added height is extremely useful.

For example, on my terrace I created a "wall" of 15-foot-high privet "trees" across one complete end

which overlooked a formidable sheer drop.
Throughout the growing season I cut away all new
sucker growth as well as any new branches on the
lower limbs. These shoots, if retained, would have
produced the usual bushy hedge, but upon their
removal the remaining trunks became stronger,
taller, and developed an appearance similar to a
clump of birches.

Masses of fragrant white flowers appear on the
uncut top branches in early summer, later becoming
dark berries which provide a feast for visiting birds.
My privet "wall" not only helps temper the winds,
but now also helps minimize the appearance of a
recently erected apartment building . . . although,
I have to admit, I never planned it that way.

suckers from
understock

However, there is one type of sucker growth which
must be removed. This is the new growth produced
directly by the "understock," or grafted root portion
of the plant.

It is common nursery practice to improve a
particular variety by grafting a desired plant top or
"scion" onto the lower stem and roots of a
stronger but related plant. This tough root stock
sometimes sends up its own shoots directly and such
growth subsequently competes with the plant *above*
the graft (which is the plant you thought you
bought). If not removed, understock suckers will
take over completely.

It is easy to spot an understock sucker on a single
stemmed plant such as a flowering crab apple or
cherry tree. However, since such suckers may also
emerge from the grafted understock of
multistemmed shrubs, like roses, a bit of detective
work may be necessary. Fortunately, this is made
easier by the fact that leaves produced on the
suckers from the understock will be *slightly different*
from those of the desired plant above. By looking

for this difference it's possible to immediately cut off the intruders.

Some understock suckers do have an annoying habit of reappearing periodically. But if they are pinched off promptly, as close to the stem as possible, they will cause no harm.

Next to be pruned are branches which crowd each other to the extent that they actually touch and *rub* when blown by the wind. This rubbing eventually causes injury to the bark and like any continually reopened wound will be vulnerable to disease or insects.

crossing branches

But occasionally, actual removal of either branch may not be necessary.

On my own terrace, because of high winds, two large branches of a newly acquired sourwood tree were destined to wreak havoc with each other. Rather than remove either one, I devised a protective shield for the limbs by enclosing them each in several inches of rubber hose slit lengthwise. So, now it's the hoses which rub each other and the bark and branches are safe.

when to prune

Anytime is the time to prune your plants for the Dead, Damaged, or Diseased wood. Immediately, if such is possible; the idea is to avoid leaving the plant in a vulnerable state for too long. However, in the middle of the winter, the pests are dormant too, so it's not necessary to brave snow and ice to remove storm-damaged branches. In general, though, very early spring or very late winter has become the classic time for the majority of normal pruning activities.

Fall is usually the poorest time to prune since food is stored in the limbs and every bit will be needed, certainly by deciduous plants, for the winter rest period. Then, too, some amount of winter kill of a

Tulips

few of the tips is inevitable, especially on windy terraces, so the longer the twig length allowed to remain (a sacrifice to the cold) the longer the length you will have left over later. In addition, studies of plant wounds indicate that they heal most quickly during the spring period of vigorous sap movement.

In the spring, impatience with the gray city weighs most heavily on the apartment dweller. Lengthening days finally devoid of winter's biting winds are reminders that summer will be . . . after all. The catalogues with their color plates of perfect plants evoke impatient glances at the still buds outside. A welcome escape from a stuffy apartment is provided since pruning is a valid excuse to venture forth.

advantages of
early spring
pruning
At this time the shape of deciduous plants is easily observed unencumbered by leaves or flowers. It is possible, too, to see where new growth will be heading.

Is the emerging form satisfactory? Do any branches rub each other? Is the center already too crowded? And careful observation will reveal the extent of the winter-killed tips.

flowering trees
and shrubs
But beginner BEWARE.

Early spring pruning of a *spring flowering* tree or shrub means also cutting off the dormant flower buds. Spring-flowering plants such as forsythia, crab apple, cherry, rhododendron, azalea, etc. have set their flower buds the previous summer. These buds are present in a dormant state awaiting the warm weather and longer days. The enthusiastic novice who chooses such a plant for his early spring pruning will have to wait till the following year to recoup his colorful loss!

On the other hand, summer flowering plants such as privet, hydrangea, spiraea, or roses make their flowers on the new or current season's wood and so it's safe to trim them in early spring.

don't cut off
the buds
The best way to avoid cutting off precious flowers before they have appeared is to prune your flowering plants immediately *after* they have flowered or right after harvesting any edible fruit. This is a general pruning rule which should see you through your most difficult times and is extemely useful whenever you are in doubt as to when the flower buds are set.

Pruning of evergreens requires a bit more knowledge of the particular species you own, general rules being harder to come by. I normally follow the previous guide with my flowering

broadleaved evergreens. (Though sometimes I
cut them just as the spring color is beginning to
show and bring the branches inside for a living
room display.) But many *needle* evergreens do not
renew themselves from the main trunk the way
broadleaved evergreens or deciduous shrubs and
trees do, so one must approach them carefully.
Severe cutting of some of these plants can be a
calamity if you don't know what you're doing.
In general, to promote bushiness it is possible to
safely cut off *half of the tip* of the newest growth in
late spring. Several new buds will eventually
emerge from this point. Pines, spruces, firs, and most
other conifers (cone-bearing trees) may be treated
in this manner but should not be cut back, by the
beginner, at least, more than that. Keep in mind
that only the shrubby type of needle evergreen such
as yews and junipers may grow entire new branches
from the older portions.

Azaleas

It would take another whole book to discuss
pruning techniques of the other types of plants you
may have on your terrace, such as espaliered,
trained, weeping, or other specimen forms, for

"pruning" is a lot more than just "cutting." The general principles outlined above will start you on your way, but, as Montague Free said in one of his books: "Pruning is a lifetime study and should be carried out thoughtfully . . ."

Many plants do have excellent powers of recuperation from a too hasty decision, but it's best, when working to achieve an attractive plant shape, to TAKE YOUR TIME.

think before you cut

Maintaining interesting-looking plants is terribly important in tiny gardens where every plant is a "specimen" plant simply because space is so limited. But in order to develop your eye and achieve the "art" of pruning, a great deal of time must be spent looking at many plants, their preferred growing habit, and then imagining their potential in your own garden.

In any case, this is where an enjoyable day may be well spent in a nearby botanic garden or arboretum. Despite their terribly tight budgets, these marvelous living "museums" manage to maintain their grounds magnificently. Their expert and devoted employees are also artists from whom a great deal may be learned. (I wish I could say the same for all of our public parks.)

As mentioned earlier, pruning has been raised to a fine art by bonsai gardeners. One can learn much by studing what they have done to control the growth of their little trees while maintaining an attractive and natural form. I am fortunate in that I live near the magnificent collection of bonsai in the Brooklyn Botanic Garden. Their outdoor Japanese garden is another special learning treat. Any season is beautiful there but the spectacular display of *small* spring flowering trees and shrubs is without rival in this area.

Maple blossoms

S. Gardner

One bonsai technique which you may find especially useful is that of "wiring." When a bonsai gardener wishes to modify the shape and/or direction of a branch, he gently bends it into the position he prefers, carefully tying it with copper wire. By maintaining it thus for several seasons, its growth becomes permanently redirected. On the terrace, since you are dealing with large branches which may be subject to high winds, this technique as such is unsuitable, but the basic idea may be adapted. Using heavy packing cord and aided by a secure base, like the terrace railing or another, strong limb, you can tie misguided, but flexible, branches into another direction and change their future growth. (As a mother, dare I say "as the twig is bent, so grows the tree"?) Quite often it is possible to retrain and avoid unnecessary cutting.

bonsai wiring

redirecting growth

I have two crab apples which periodically like to send out horizontal, eye-level branches. It is most distressing to contemplate removing these marvelous flowering limbs. But I also prefer not to get my eyes gouged out. Moving the trees to another section of the terrace is an alternative solution, but I like them where they are. So several years ago I chose to borrow this bonsai idea and redirect their growth, vertically. By tying together two branches from opposite sides, each branch pulled the other upward and literally solved the problem of two birds with one stone. Over the years new branches must be trained as the original ties are removed. The redirected branches remain where they are positioned and are no longer lethal.

One day in early spring, I glanced up at the terrace of a neighbor and was horrified to see him balanced on his railing frenetically hacking away at his birch tree. The reason for his mighty struggle was that he

the proper
shears for the
job

was attempting to prune it with a set of hedge
shears. It should have been obvious that such an
instrument affords neither the proper control, nor
the proper cut for this kind of job, as he really was
having a time of it.

Now it is true that the cost of maintaining even the
smallest balcony can become considerable.

However, there are some things that even the
tiniest garden must have, and these include a set of
well-sharpened hand pruners.

In addition, if there are trees of any height at all, an
investment in a long-handled pruner or lobber is
also justified. This will permit cutting through
diameters up to about 1½ inches.

Since plants in tubs are already several feet above
the floor, a tall-growing variety may reach
considerable height and far out over the street,
many stories below. If you own any extremely tall
plants, you might consider investing in a pole
pruner. This will extend your treetop reach to
between 12 and 15 feet, and more if you have the
courage to climb onto a chair as well. But there is a
limit as to how high even the bravest, most devoted
terrace gardener can safely venture on a kitchen
stepstool, and then actually succeed in removing top
dead branches. Country gardeners hire tree

companies to climb up and do the job for them, a most unlikely proposition for those in high-rise buildings however.

At a certain point, then, it becomes necessary to accept the fact that some of those branches are simply out of safe reach and try to ignore them. In pliable specimens, such as willows or birches, it is sometimes possible to bend the offending limb sufficiently to reach the top with a pruner. This is no easy matter and, unless a sympathetic friend helps, can prove more frustrating than successful. In such cases, rather than risk a plunge over the side, it's better to leave the top of the tree alone and hope some strong wind eventually does the pruning instead.

hard-to-reach branches

Occasionally there are some really thick branches which may require removal. The terrace gardener must resist the impulse to run to his tool kit and drag out the largest saw. A carpenter's saw was not designed with tree pruning in mind and has the wrong teeth and the wrong shape for this job. If there are many mature trees or shrubs on your terrace, it is wise to purchase a proper tree saw, as well as study the books which discuss the procedure for removing large limbs without damaging the bark. Tree saws are fairly inexpensive and available at garden centers. Some even fold safely into a compact, storable shape.

dealing with large branches

However, for ordinary terrace maintenance, a set of well-sharpened hand pruners should hold you for a while.

An open wound on any living thing is an invitation to trouble . . . and for many years it has been assumed that plants are no exception. Thus, a sealer of "tree paint," as it is commonly called, has been a must for woody plants. An already mixed compound to seal and protect the opening is available in small aerosol cans. These are quite convenient for terrace work, and experienced gardeners recommend painting any wound larger than a dime. Being rather conservative, I automatically apply it to any cut I make on a woody plant.

And this includes the time I broke the bark of my birch tree when I hit it with a broom handle. This accident occurred during an instance of emotional overkill when I discovered the twenty-third caterpillar of the season climbing up the tree and the broom was the first thing I could grab.

This is hardly an approved method of pest control but I did then seal the wound properly with "tree paint." (My aim and control improved for the next shot.) Recently, however, according to a bulletin from the American Horticultural Society, scientists found that tree wounds healed as fast or faster when not treated and that plain shellac seemed superior to the "usual gooey black stuff." As of this writing, though, the outcome is not yet determined and I am unqualified to comment. I do have an opinion (of course) and since I feel better if I put some sort of protection on the cut, I shall continue to do so until more evidence comes to hand.

As your interest in pruning develops, it is a good idea to refer to one of the many books devoted exclusively to the subject (see Bibliography) although the principles outlined here should suffice for the beginner.

In any event, while an overly enthusiastic pruning may test the plant kingdom's amazing recuperative powers, it is more likely that it will not be the gardeners but the doctors (and their "evil surgical operations") who must "bury their mistakes."

PRUNING
MAKES THE
MOST OF THE
NATURALLY
GRACEFUL
HABIT OF A
RUSSIAN OLIVE

EVEN
NORMALLY
LARGE TREES
LIKE THIS
WILLOW
WILL BE
HAPPY ON
SMALL
TERRACES IF
THEY ARE
THEY ARE KEPT
WELL PRUNED

Regret for spring's passing—
year after year, and yet
never the same.
Gekkyō

Section 10

The Established Garden—Keep It Going

No gardener can afford to rest on his laurels.
No matter the size or location, every garden needs
continued attention in order to remain healthy and
beautiful. During the time spent writing this book I
saw several of the terraces I had already
photographed fade and die when their original
owners moved away. All too often the new
occupants approached their freshly acquired garden
armed only with love.
Unfortunately this is not always quite enough.
So although the "established garden" discussed in
this section may be your own of several seasons, it
may also be one you have just acquired by virtue of a
change of address.
This section was not intended for the gardener who
is just beginning, but new owners of existing terraces
may have to plunge in anyway.

the older
garden,
"inherited"
or otherwise

To begin with, it is important to realize that as *any*
cultivated plant (tree or houseplant) makes use of
the nutrients in its original soil, those nutrients must
be restored or rebalanced with man's help. Also,
even the best soil mix eventually begins to lose
its original porosity and friable, granular structure.
This reduces the availability of air and water
around the roots. On a small scale, you may have

soil
impoverish-
ment is
inevitable

noticed this in your little houseplants. But both nutrient depletion and soil compaction can occur on a large scale in suburban gardens and even huge farms.

Soil will not rejuvenate itself all alone by magic. Our gardening is unique in that it combines the growing of mature trees and shrubs with the "houseplant" conditions of restricted containers. You may think your terrace's big planters are enormous, but they are containers, after all.

Soil which has become barren or compact eventually causes the plant's decline. Early signs of this may be a decrease in the size and number of new leaves, a paling of the general color tone, and a decrease or total lack of flowers or fruit. Sometimes when this happens people shrug and say, "Well, that plant just can't take the city!" It may never occur to them that the plant is simply beginning to show signs of the *deficiency* or *unavailability* of nutrients and water.

some early signs of decline

In order to keep your established garden going, then, you must restore the soil. If your garden has been treated to any previous cultivation (such as discussed in Section 8) you are already ahead of the game. Otherwise, you have a bit of work before you in order to catch up. In any case, it is important first to understand a little of what the soil nutrients are and what they do.

All members of the plant kingdom (even insect-eaters and other strange jungle residents) require 3 *main* substances for good general health. These are:

npk, the big three

NITROGEN—PHOSPHORUS—POTASH (potassium)
Each affects the well-being of plants in many ways, but summarized briefly they are:

NITROGEN (N)   imparts a healthy green glow
                  to the leaves and encourages
                  lush growth.
PHOSPHORUS (P)   stimulates flowering and
                  setting of fruit and encourages
                  good root formation.
POTASH (K)   imparts general hardiness,
                  disease resistance, and vigor.

"vitamin pills" for plants

Just as man derives "food" benefit from both "nutritious, well-balanced meals" and supplementary "vitamin pills," there are several ways to "feed" your plants.* Making use of this analogy, we might say that the "vitamin pills" for plants are the synthetic chemical fertilizers which abound on the shelves of garden shops. Their convenience and practicality for our tiny gardens are not to be disparaged. But it is important to keep in mind that just as with vitamin pills for humans, chemical fertilizers must be regarded as *supplements* to an otherwise sensible diet and are not to be used to the exclusion of other beneficial "food." (And more importantly, chemical fertilizers will not restore the soil structure.)

chemical fertilizers

There are many chemical fertilizers available, each claiming more miracles than the other. Thus the only way to figure out what is best for which plant is to *carefully* read the label. The most important item you will see on the package (of any fertilizer) is a set of three hyphenated numbers. These refer to the percentage of the big three nutrients, in order:

* Actually it is misleading to say that we must "feed" plants. We only supply the substances from which green plants make their own food.

Before buying anything, then, decide first what you
are trying to do. If, for example, you need to give a
"general feeding," select a fertilizer in which all
three numbers are the same, such as 10–10–10.
But, if you wish to give special encouragement, say,
to your flowering shrubs and trees, then select a
fertilizer higher in phosphorus (to boost flower
stimulation). Since the phosphorus percentage is
represented by the middle number in the set, the
fertilizer to select is one where this central figure is
higher than the other two, such as 10–15–10.

interpreting
the label

Some chemical fertilizers may be worked directly
into the soil. Others, such as "Ra-pid-Gro®,"
"Hyponex®," or Stern's "Miracle-Gro®," must
first be dissolved and diluted in water. Some are
recommended for use on leaves directly. Still others
have a controlled-release action and dissolve in the
soil by themselves over several months.
I prefer those which I measure and dilute first with
water, since I feel that gives me better control of the
distribution throughout the container.
Whatever you choose, though, *never never* exceed
the recommended dosages or proportion of water
mix. This is not a case where if a little is good a lot
will be better.
"A lot" can result in death . . . so don't do it!
Read that entire label carefully and adhere
faithfully to the directions. If you still have some
doubts, lean to the stingy side and remember that
"less is more."
Because many synthetic fertilizers produce rapid
results (except for the controlled-release types),
the plant may respond soon after application. In the
spring or through midsummer this is fine. But as the
days begin to shorten and the outdoor trees and
shrubs in cold climates prepare to enter a resting

applying
chemical
fertilizers

period, their systems begin to slow down. The new growth may not have a chance to develop sufficiently to withstand the cold. Therefore, don't use fast-acting fertilizers in the late summer or fall. (Here in New York I stop by about the third week in August.)

trace elements

In addition to the Big 3, Nitrogen-Phosphorus-Potash, scientists have discovered that there are well over a dozen other nutrients also necessary to the health of plants, foremost among which is iron. These are known collectively as "trace elements" because they are often required in extremely small quantities. For this reason it is difficult for us to deal with them specifically in our containers despite the fact that their lack can cause problems.

How convenient it is, then, that some fertilizer manufacturers also include a small quantity of what they usually call "secondary plant foods" (although that is a dubious phrase). If you read the labels carefully, in addition to iron you may find listed there such delicacies as calcium, manganese, zinc, boron, molybdenum, etc. But because the amount of trace elements required by each plant is still unclear, it is not a good idea to wantonly add them in all the time.

serving well-balanced meals

And since this is one of the objections to relying only on "vitamin pills," let's return to our analogy and take a look now at the other food source. "nutritious well-balanced meals."

restoring organic matter to the soil

Just like man, plants benefit greatly when treated to vitamins naturally found in organic and mineral matter. It would be an understatement to say that such matter is an extremely important part of *any* garden. Only through the use of such materials are we able to restore to the soil not only matter needed by the plant to manufacture its food, but the original *good structure* as well.

Only by such restoration may we create a truly *fertile* soil, one rich with live, healthy organisms. It is the continual activity of this microscopic life which improves soil structure and makes possible the penetration of both water and air. A garden where no effort has been made to restore the soil in this sense is living on borrowed time. No amount of chemical feeding will change this simple fact.

spring
restoration

Thus in the spring, once the soil has thawed and dried so that it's no longer soggy wet, it's important to get outside and do a little digging-in of organic substances. Very early spring is best for this, not only because the gardener is rested after his own winter dormancy (and can face the work) but because the trees and shrubs are just getting ready to begin their active growing period.

humus-making
substances

The first substance to add to your tubs is an "all-purpose" humus-making fertilizer. The word "humus," so favored by gardeners, is a peculiar one and sometimes hard for the beginner to understand. The rich "humusy" soil found in the forest is the result of years of decomposing plant (and animal) matter like leaves, stems, roots, etc. The decomposition occurred because of the activity of microorganisms.

Our tubs are so limited in size that we cannot duplicate the conditions under which enough humus is formed; certainly not at the rate at which it is needed. Thus, we must continually add matter which the soil will be able to use while it is also making its own. Ideal for this is well-rotted *leaf mold* or *compost,* and lucky the terrace owner who has room (or a friend who has room) to make some himself. I don't. But fortunately my local garden center now carries these vital materials.

If you are unable to find such a supplier, don't despair. It is possible to substitute well-rotted *barnyard* or *cow manure* and small packages of these products are relatively easy to buy. Their "fertilizer" property is less important than the environment they create for encouraging the activity of microorganisms which help restore the soil.

There is no cookbook-recipe amount one "should" use but I work in a generous handful for each 2 feet or so of plant height, more or less.

If the soil in your tubs has become quite compacted, it is also time for several generous trowels of perlite mixed with peat moss. This helps improve the drainage and aeration. For older tubs, some limestone may have to be added, but more about that later.

Next to be restored, and easily found at garden centers, are organic and mineral sources of the "Big 3" mentioned previously. You may ask: "Am I not supplying them when I apply my chemical fertilizers?" Yes, but, restating the analogy, your chemical fertilizers are like "vitamin pills" and do not produce the rich, fertile soil such as results from "serving well-balanced meals."

By providing organic and mineral sources of the required nutrients, you come closer to truly "nutritious food" for your plants. And if done with care, the need for "pills," then, will be minimal.

Nitrogen, the first of the Big 3 needed by plants, is also the first of the Big 3 to leach out and disappear from the soil.

Several organic materials which are especially high in nitrogen are:

> blood meal
> fish emulsion
> soybean meal
> cottonseed meal

Phosphorus, so vital for flowering and fruit set and also the next likely to be deficient, is found to a large degree in:

> bone meal
> superphosphate
> rock phosphate
> oyster meal

Potash (or Potassium), often least likely to be in short supply in your soil, may be found in:

> wood ashes
> seaweed
> kelp
> potash rock
> potassium sulphate

how much to
add?

The question of "exactly" how much of each of the Big 3 to use cannot be answered precisely unless you have a resident scientist running tests and advising you continually. But a major advantage to using nutrients derived from natural sources is that a fatal overdose such as that caused by careless use of synthetics is less likely to occur.

First of all, check the label for a recommended amount and, if you're lucky, you'll find directions you can follow easily. Unfortunately, some labels have an annoying habit of suggesting application in terms of acres or hundreds of square feet. I wasn't the first to be unnerved by this, though, and in a pamphlet written by soil scientist Dr. Charles E. Kellogg for the USDA, these figures have been recomputed, making them useful for application in small gardens. I have adapted the chart on acres here for use on terraces. (Although first issued in 1945, his pamphlet entitled "How Much Fertilizer Shall I Use?" is timely and in wide use today.)

But to begin with, you must get the area of your container. If you find math terrifying, chances are you will not kill your large trees or shrubs by adding only a handful to each plant tub. However, it is quite easy to figure out the area or square footage of your containers and then use the proportionate amount recommended on the package. To find the area, just multiply the length by the width. If the container is round, you can use the formula for area (which is: $3.14 \times r^2$) or just multiply half of its diameter by itself and then that answer by 3. That's all. Your container's height is *not* a factor. (Plants are supposed to be growing in the ground, remember?) Then you can use the following chart or maybe even the label.

computing the area of containers

IF THE QUANTITY SUGGESTED PER ACRE IS:	1,000 lbs.	300 lbs.	100 lbs.	44 lbs.
Use in A CONTAINER OF 100 sq. ft. (2½ ft. by 40 ft.)	2¼ lbs.	11 ounces	3½ ounces	1½ ounces
Use in A CONTAINER OF 25 sq. ft. (2½ ft. by 10 ft.)	1¼ cup	6 tablespoons	2 tablespoons	1 tablespoon
Use in A CONTAINER OF 5 sq. ft. (2 ft. by 2½ ft.)	4 tablespoons	1 tablespoon	1¼ teaspoon	½ teaspoon
Use in A CONTAINER OF 2½ sq. ft. (2 ft. by 1½ ft.)	2 tablespoons	1½ teaspoons	½ teaspoon	¼ teaspoon

So, in the spring, with all your supplies purchased and laid out before you, rework your tubs by digging in and down, adding what is needed all around. Loosen the soil and don't be afraid of breaking some roots.

dig in and . . .

Yes, the restoration process now will actually entail breaking some roots!

As implied previously and shocking as it sounds, purposely breaking or cutting some roots is exactly what must be done periodically as part of the maintenance of the established terrace garden. Such heresy.

You may well ask, where did this idea come from and how can such a thing be done? Well, as you may know, houseplants must periodically be transplanted into larger containers when they become potbound. Our outdoor trees and shrubs are also in containers.

want to repot a tree?

Does that mean that as they get older and bigger we must take them out and repot them too?

Even with houseplants, there is a point beyond which one cannot possibly repot and still be considered sane. And that is assuming one can even lift the larger plants in the first place. Obviously, another solution is needed.

When I reached this impasse originally, I decided to turn for inspiration to those masters of container trees and shrubs, the bonsai gardeners. Many of the big plants on my terrace were the same or similar to species I had seen in the bonsai collection at the Brooklyn Botanic Garden. The only difference was size: size of containers (mine were bigger) and size of plants (mine were bigger, again).

I learned that bonsai trees and shrubs are *root-pruned* . . . and therefore perhaps I should do likewise. The question then was "How?"

root pruning, bonsai-style

Root pruning, or the cutting of roots of trees and shrubs, has been practiced by bonsai gardeners for hundreds of years. They remove the little plants from their containers, cut some of the older roots, and then, along with renewed soil, return them to the *very same pot*. This results in two important accomplishments.

First, new root growth is encouraged: a vital event because old roots are mostly passageways and it is the fine young roots which absorb the water and nutrients for the plant.

dwarfing large plants but keeping them happy

Second, by having their roots cut periodically, the trees and shrubs are kept dwarfed. Thus they remain happy in their confined containers and limited growing space despite the fact that in their *natural* state (in the forest or countryside), such species could grow quite large.

I heard first that some bonsai gardeners merely chop straight across all the roots, equidistant from the trunk in all directions. This seemed a bit severe and was an interesting beginning. But it soon became apparent that the majority of bonsai practitioners were more meticulous and actually took pains to disentangle the root ball, cutting carefully and more selectively.

Swell.

But I was still not about to take my 10- and 12-foot-high trees out of their containers! It was evidently going to be impossible for me to follow bonsai procedure literally (even though I was advised by an expert I spoke with to "hire a crane and do it right" . . . experts are sometimes helpful like that). Then I realized that the root-pruning *idea* could be utilized by approaching the job from another direction, namely, from *above*. And of course this is just what we are starting to do anyway, as we dig into the tubs in order to restore nutrients to the soil! All we have to do is go down a lot farther.

root pruning, terrace-style

Therefore, in the spring, before the new leaves break, start at the outermost portion of one side of the planter and dig down firmly with sharp jabbing motions here and there. It's best to do this with a narrow shovel or spade which is quite sharp. Hand tools may not be convenient for the taller tubs, so this is the time to buy some long-handled ones as well as a sharpening stone or file. As sections of the roots are cut, reach in and pull out the mass. Observe how tightly packed the roots are on your different plant types.

From each of the larger and older trees and shrubs where the roots are dense remove a total of about a half dozen good-sized bunches; from the smaller or younger ones, remove less.

When root-pruning your established plants for the first time, it's best to work on only two opposite sides of the container and leave the other two for the following year. After the initial two years or so of this type of deep root pruning, use your judgment (based on how densely packed the roots seem to be) as to how often the practice should be repeated. In general, I am guided by the "schedule" followed by many bonsai gardeners, which is to root-prune:

how often
NEEDLE EVERGREENS . . . every 3 to
5 years
BROADLEAVED EVERGREENS . . . every
3 or 4
years
FLOWERING OR FRUITING DECIDUOUS TREES
. . . every
2 or 3
years

The first time you dig into your older, very fast-growing plants such as privets, willows, and some vines, you may find they have virtually no soil left at all and are just a mass of roots. In such cases, you will have quite a job to get them back in some semblance of control. (I never quite manage much more than a "semblance" myself.) These types, therefore, can be *slightly* root-pruned at least every year.

Once the bonsai gardener is finished with cutting the roots, he then proceeds to cut back some of the upper parts of the plant as well. This is to keep it *dwarfed* as well as looking as it should, based on his training in the tradition of classic styles and shapes. But it is also because with some of the roots eliminated, the aboveground parts of the plant receive a reduced amount of nutrients and water. Therefore, you too must prune away some of the branches. But not being restricted to classic art forms, and since for your purposes a "dwarfed" plant might be quite large, you can be more flexible in both how and when you do this.

compensation top pruning

Quite often, I find that I've done my top pruning before the root pruning, simply because cold weather in the spring often delays soil work but does not prevent pruning work.

top pruning before root pruning

If you have not yet done so, then, this is the time to catch up on some of the general pruning as discussed in the preceding section. If an early flowering tree or shrub is involved (and you don't want to cut off those unopened buds), it is possible to delay the top branch pruning until right after the plant has flowered. It is also possible to cut the branches anyway and bring them inside for forcing into flower. (Such "forcing" means just putting the branches in a nice vase with water and waiting.) In any case, be sure to watch your recently root-pruned plants carefully as the spring progresses. If you have not cut *enough* top branches to compensate for the root loss, the new leaves may appear at first, but shortly thereafter some branch endings will begin to droop significantly. This will be a signal to quickly cut away more, removing either several large branches, lots of smaller ones, or just many of the ends. In any

signs of insufficient cutting

case, remember to keep all your plants properly watered during the period of early spring growth.

As the gardener continues his quest for further knowledge, he soon notices references being made to pH or the "degree of acidity or alkalinity" of the soil.

the mystery of
acidity and
alkalinity
When I reached this point myself (never having studied chemistry), I began to fear that with the mysteries of the soil locked in erudite volumes, my terrace would be a disaster where no self-respecting plant would live.

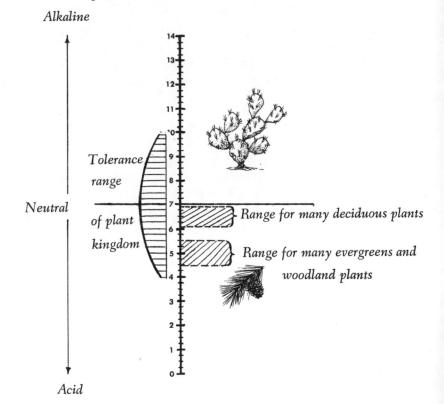

Alkaline

Neutral

Acid

Tolerance range of plant kingdom

Range for many deciduous plants

Range for many evergreens and woodland plants

14
13
12
11
10
9
8
7
6
5
4
3
2
1
0

THE pH SCALE

As the years passed and nothing too dreadful happened, I felt a great relief, needless to say. However, as the years passed and I grew more interested in having a better garden, it became apparent that some acquaintance with the pH factor would be useful. And it was not nearly as complicated as I had feared.

Explained simply, soils in their natural state vary in their chemical composition. These chemicals alter the alkalinity or acidity of the soil. This in turn affects the nutrients present in that soil, making them more *or* less available for different plant species.

the pH scale Chemists have conveniently devised a scale of numbers from 1 to 14, sort of like a thermometer, which indicates amounts of acidity or alkalinity (technically called the hydrogen ion concentration). The acid-alkaline relationship has as its universal symbol the two letters pH, written just like that. (The intervals of the scale are split in many subdivisions but the minutiae are of little importance to gardeners.)

As shown in the illustration, 7 is "neutral." Below 7 is acid and above 7 is alkaline.

An example of an acid substance in the home is vinegar or grapefruit, while an alkaline substance is baking soda. Distilled water is considered neutral.

Some plants found growing in the desert, such as certain cacti, are tolerant of very alkaline soils, which may have a pH range of up to 9. Some plants found deep within a peat bog forest, such as certain pines, are tolerant of very acid soils, which may have a pH range down to about 4. But these are very extreme and are of interest only to give an idea of the types of plant conditions found at each end of this spectrum.

Generally speaking, it is quite unlikely that species tolerant of such extremes will be encountered by the average gardener. The majority of plants ordinarily found at most garden centers do well in a soil range which is in the area just below neutral (or around pH 6 to 6.5). The last column in the Tree and Shrub List in Section 3 will give you an idea of the soil conditions tolerated by some common terrace species.

general soil tolerance

If you wish to learn more about the pH of the soil in your planters, it is possible to mail a soil sample to the county extension office of the State University Agricultural School nearest you.

If you feel scientific, though, inexpensive soil-testing kits are available and you can give it a try yourself. While not exceptionally accurate, these kits generally will be good enough for your purposes.

analyze your soil yourself

The most common ones come with a color chart and small jars of liquid chemicals. The procedure often entails mixing a small amount of one of the chemicals with a teaspoon or so of soil. The resulting color is then compared with that shown on the chart, which may be labeled acid, neutral, alkaline, etc. In any case, be sure to read and follow the directions on the particular kit you buy. Once you gain the knack, you may find it as much fun as I do and invest in still more expensive and elaborate kits and meters to test for the various soil properties. Many soil-test kits are available at garden centers but it is also possible to order them by mail. One place you can write for a catalogue of these is the Sudbury Laboratory, Inc., P. O. Box 1264, Sudbury, Mass. 01766.

As I said before, many garden plants will be fine in a soil just to the acid side of neutral. Our basic soil recipe (Section 5) should yield a soil in this area or

altering the pH

somewhat lower, depending on the type of peat moss used.

But in any case, soil in the eastern part of the United States, and in many large cities, has a tendency with time to become more acid. This is fine for plants which tolerate a distinctly acid reaction such as many evergreens and other woodland plants. And if you need to help the process along, the pH may be lowered still further by the addition of aluminum sulphate or iron sulphate, which may be found in garden centers. Follow the directions on the package, leaning to the conservative side. Frugal applications over several seasons are better than a single massive overdose, which can shock the plant's system.

acidifying the soil

However, many plants will not be so happy when the pH value of their soil gets too low and you may find yourself spending more time trying to raise this level than lower it.

Gardeners have found that by working limestone into the soil, this change is easily effected. Once again, adapting Dr. Kellogg's charts, we have the following guide for doing this (assuming an average soil mix):

LIMESTONE REQUIRED TO RAISE THE pH .5

PLANT CONTAINERS SIZED APPROXIMATELY:	WILL NEED ABOUT:
100 square feet (such as 2½ ft. X 40 ft.)	4½ lbs. of limestone
25 square feet (such as 2½ ft. X 10 ft.)	2½ cups of limestone
5 square feet (such as 2 ft. X 2½ ft.)	½ cup of limestone
2½ square feet (such as 2 ft. X ½ ft.)	¼ cup of limestone

For very heavy soils, slightly more limestone will be required; for light soils, less. Again, stay on the frugal side and don't try to raise the pH drastically in one season.

the pH of
some garden
materials

Of great interest to me is the pH reaction of some common garden materials as listed in one of my favorite reference works, Taylor's Encyclopedia. These are:

Lime . . . . pH	12.0
Bone Meal	10.0
Ashes	9.0
Animal Manures .	8.0
Coffee Grounds and Tea Leaves . . .	5.0
Cottonseed Meal .	4.5
Peat Moss	4.0
Aluminum Sulphate	3.2
Superphosphate . .	2.0

It is apparent, then, that during the normal course of your gardening you will be changing the pH of your soil slightly as you work in the different fertilizing or reconditioning materials.

Sometimes, with many plants on your terrace to take care of, all the things I've talked of doing in this section can add up . . . and one can easily get hopelessly confused and forget what has or has not been done and when!

what to do and
when

As the plant life on my terrace multiplied, I found this happening to me and started keeping an "almanac" of gardening activities. A structured program of sorts evolved, as I found that certain things were being done more or less at the same time each year (either out of convenience for me, or timeliness for the plants). Although different organic and mineral sources are sometimes substituted, a routine program for keeping my garden in good health often is as follows:

a useful health
program to
follow

TIME OF YEAR:	EARLY SPRING	EARLY SUMMER	AUTUMN
	(in April or when the ground is easily workable and not soggy wet)	(late May or early June, when the bulk of annuals appear at local garden centers)	(mid-October or when deciduous leaves begin to fall)
WORK DONE	1. top-branch pruning. 2. remove winter mulch of evergreen boughs, leaving loose needles on the soil 3. thoroughly loosen soil and rework all tubs 4. root prune as required (compensation top pruning where needed)	1. gently and lightly loosen uppermost layer of soil in all tubs containing non-evergreen trees and shrubs 2. add first batch of summer flowers	1. remove all spent summer flowers 2. loosen and rework soil in all tubs 3. add spring bulbs 4. add evergreen boughs when available during holidays
NUTRIENTS ADDED	cow manure or compost (well rotted only) for all tubs superphosphate for tubs with fruiting, flowering trees, shrubs and vines bloodmeal for all tubs with nonflowering trees and shrubs	superphosphate for all tubs with flowering trees, shrubs and vines liquid chemical fertilizers for all tubs, a dilute, "all-purpose" mixture (2 or 3 times through the summer)	lime for tubs where need is indicated cow manure all tubs where lime has not been added or compost for all tubs bone meal for all tubs perlite where need is indicated

One final word about the established garden. In Section 2 I discussed understanding one's own garden "climate" as well as the fact that plants are alive and thus constantly changing. As they grow they may alter some of the original conditions you observed. For example, taller trees may now be filtering or otherwise blocking the light which was available previously.

It is useful to be aware of these changes and the effect on new introductions as well as older residents. Periodically, then, look at your established garden just as suggested in that section.

You might be surprised at what you see there.

changed microclimates

SOME USEFUL
PRODUCTS ON
DISPLAY AT A
NURSERY

PLANTS
WHICH ARE
NOT
ROOT-PRUNED
EVENTUALLY
BECOME
COMPLETELY
POTBOUND
LIKE THIS
LARGE PRIVET

ROOT PRUNING
"TERRACE-
STYLE":
REMOVE
SEVERAL
HANDFULS OF
ROOTS

Insects one hears—
and one hears the talk of men—
with different ears.

Wafū

Section 11

A Word About the Birds and Bees

Yes, Virginia, there are birds and bees in the middle of cities.
And few city sounds are more glorious than birds chirping just outside the window; few city sights more fascinating than bees around a flower. Both the birds and the bees are sure to be attracted by your oasis of plant life they spot from on high. If you want to maintain a "real" garden you will not wish to keep them away.

The birds may come first, looking for insects, seeds, or fruit as well as a safe spot to rest. As with any guest, a sign of your hospitality is the offering of food, which tells them they are welcome to return. Since a terrace has but limited natural supply, you will have to provide them with additional food.

the welcome mat for wild birds

The easiest way to begin your bird feeding is by placing some parakeet "seed trees" throughout the garden. These are available at many supermarkets, pet shops or dime stores. Using a string or rubber band, it's easy to tie them onto the railing, fence, or among larger tree or shrub branches.

The birds become "trained" to revisit when they start to remember where free food is available. Early spring is probably the easiest time in which to succeed in attracting them on a regular basis, but a delay of several weeks or more before they come or before you see them eating, is quite common. So don't get discouraged. But do eliminate any thoughts you may have about tossing bread or other table scraps onto the floor. Cockroaches, pigeons, or other undesirables may well arrive first.

Once you succeed in attracting a few steady customers you can select the best location for installing a permanent bird feeder (or more than one if the terrace is large) based on your observation of the feeding spots most popular. Although buying a wild bird feeder in a large city can be something of a treasure hunt, check the pet shops of big department stores, the zoo, or the botanic gardens. In all likelihood the best selection will be found at a suburban garden center, although some lovely items are also available through mail-order catalogues. One such brochure which is most helpful indeed is from a company which specializes in wild bird products called Duncraft. You can receive their free booklet by writing them at 25 S. Main St., Penacooke, N.H. 03301.

the feeder and the food

The most common feeders are made for loose seed. Select one which is easy to fill, easy to hang (or to attach to the railing or wall), and has place for more than one bird to stand. On my own terrace, the most successful feeders are those which enable birds to eat while perched on a dowel-stick-shaped support. These types also reduce the chance of attracting city pigeons, which apparently are a "feed-while-standing-flat" type and don't like to use a perch.
In the winter, in addition to loose seed, beef suet is another much enjoyed food. Your butcher can cut some for you or ready-made suet cakes with seed

grains mixed in can be found at garden shops.
(Where suet holders may be bought as well.)
One especially useful product I've found is called a
"Wild Bird Bell." It combines several types of seed
with corn syrup, dextrose, and fat in a solid
bell-shaped mass equipped with a hook for easy
hanging. I found it at my supermarket but if you
don't come across it locally, write to the
manufacturer: Dahlgren & Co. in Crookston,
Minnesota 56716.

I've noticed there are several reasons why sometimes
bird feeders "don't work."

why some
feeders "don't
work"

Foremost among these is the feeder's location on the
terrace. Wild birds seem to be more comfortable
eating in a relatively sheltered spot. They like to be
close to the protective branches of at least one bushy
shrub or tree where they may readily flee. After all,
city living isn't easy for birds either, so you can
understand their obsession with security.
In addition, they seem to prefer a minimum of
wind and a maximum of sun, where possible.
When these preferences of the birds conflict with
those of the terrace owner, who is only interested
in watching birds eat, both parties are bound to
suffer.
Some feeders may fail to attract, also, because they
are not comfortable for the majority of local species

cater to local
species first

to feed from. Although many birds can be found in
nearby large parks or botanic gardens, there is no
doubt that it is the sparrows and finches who are in
the majority around New York City. I have seen
others on my terrace, but apparently it is to this
majority I must cater first.

Any good-sized grouping of plants which produces
fruit, seeds, or gives shelter to insects will attract
the birds. Some plants which seem to be especially

specially liked plants

favored are:

dogwood
shadblow
holly
barberry
privet
firethorn
blueberry

But problems may arise if you want to have all the berries on the plants for yourself . . . either to look at or eat. If you do, be sure to keep a very well-stocked feeder close at hand. Bells, wind-chimes or hanging pieces of shiny metal in the plant at fruiting time will also help to keep them out. (Something I learned about one autumn after every single berry was eaten off my firethorn.)

once you start don't stop

Thoughout most of the year, I maintain several feeding areas of both loose seed and suet. The birds which remain here through the cold weather seem to rely on me as a source of winter food. But in the summer, in order to minimize the seed hulks or droppings on the floor, I use only a few parakeet seed trees, placed among the branches. This reminds them that food is available here, but in the summer they can make use of other sources as well.

water

Another way to keep birds interested in your garden is by providing fresh water. More than bathing, it is water for drinking which they need most of the time. A shallow bowl of tepid water when the weather hovers around freezing is a welcome gift indeed. I've noticed that the birds enjoy both drinking and bathing in the puddles on my terrace floor after I water my plants. They completely ignore a lovely, elaborate ceramic birdbath on a sparsely planted terrace not 50 feet away. Apparently the jungle-like atmosphere surrounding my puddles appeals to them more than the austere, foliage-free surroundings nearby.

Unless your terrace is really very large (or heavily planted) you may as well not bother providing birdhouses. Few security-conscious city birds will nest quite that close to humans. While they will find bits of things on your terrace to use for their nests, chances are they will build them elsewhere.

Once you realize that birds belong in your garden, you will not fail to realize that bees do too. I'll admit that sometimes they make me nervous, but I try to accept them as part of the larger scheme of things and hope you'll eventually agree.

the buzzin' of the bees

The bees you'll find around your flowers will be mostly hard-working bumble bees and possibly honey bees. They are entirely different from the ill-tempered wasps, hornets, or yellow jackets often found at park picnic grounds.

A specialist in the field, Dr. Jerome Rozen, Jr. (Curator of Hymenoptera at The American Museum of Natural History), assured me that most of the bees I see on my terrace are interested in the flowers only . . . not in me. They visit the flowers in order to get the nectar and sugars. Simultaneously, of course, they are helping by spreading the pollen.

Wasps, hornets, and yellow jackets are less interested in such ethereal activities and thus are more apt to bother humans. Luckily, however, they are also more apt to spend their days elsewhere, and thank goodness for that.

Another devotee of bees, who lives right in the middle of Manhattan, is hobbyist Thomas B. Congdon. Possibly the only apiculturist here, he raises honey bees in his den, where they come and go through a special opening.

He insists that these are very "gentle" creatures and that's a direct quote. Since he's willing to share his family's home with them, I certainly can't doubt his observations.

they're "gentle" creatures

And, if you spend some time watching the bees on your terrace, it soon becomes apparent that if left alone bees do humans no harm. In fact, unless you are practically in their hive or make an attempt to crush or press them directly, the possibility of being stung is quite remote. In other words, don't swat them as if they were mosquitoes. Their only interest is your plants.

Although the chances are slim that a nest or hive will be built on your terrace, if one should be, do not attempt to remove it yourself. Instead, contact the nearest zoo or other institution (Appendix 2) for the name of someone with appropriate experience to tackle the job for you.

If you should be stung, do not attempt to pull the stinger straight out directly, since it's slightly barbed and may break. Instead, use your fingernail to lead it out gently, sideways. A normal sting produces some localized pain and swelling. But a few people may have an extreme allergic reaction. This can consist of nausea, rapid, shallow breathing, paleness, or fainting. It's best to contact your doctor immediately, if you've never been stung before.

stings

The most active period for busy bees is the same as that for most busy workers: 9 to 5. (Surely there's a moral there someplace.) And like office workers, they often pause to enjoy a midday break.

On dark, cold, or rainy days, they are not too interested in working and generally take time off. (Is it possible . . . a union for bees?)

But even knowing that it's not people who interest them, many amateur gardeners are a bit disconcerted by the presence of bees on their little

"how doth the busy little bee"

terraces. If you wish to take some extra measures
to insure their lack of interest in you while you're
at work outside, wear very light-colored or white
clothing, don't make sudden very sharp moves,
avoid wearing perfume, and try to be freshly
bathed . . . even if you are working with cow
manure. Ordinary insect repellents such as "6-12"
may make you feel less apprehensive but aren't
really needed.

Probably because of jokes about the "birds and
bees," then, some people, especially in the city,
tend to forget that these creatures are part of
nature's plan and serve other functions besides
helping children learn the facts of life.
If you intend, truly, to have a garden, you will not
discourage but delight in their presence.

A WINTER
BREAKFAST IS
ENJOYED BY
BIRDS
IN THE BARE
BRANCHES OF
A JAPANESE
DOGWOOD

THESE BIRDS
ARE SITTING
OUT THE RAIN
UNDER AN
AWNING. THEY
APPARENTLY
FIND THE
WEEPING
TREE'S
BRANCHES A
GOOD PLACE
TO WAIT

BUSY LITTLE
BEES REALLY
ARE, AND
THEY WON'T
BOTHER YOU
IF YOU DON'T
BOTHER THEM.
THIS ONE IS
VISITING A
MARIGOLD

A PROFUSION
OF BLUEBERRY
FLOWERS,
WITH THE
HELP OF
FRIENDLY
BEES, WILL
YIELD PINTS
OF
DELICIOUS
FRUIT

A Gardener's Prayer

O Lord, grant that in some way
it may rain every day,
say from about midnight until three o'clock in the
    morning,
but, You see, it must be gentle and warm
so that it can soak in;
grant that at the same time it would not rain on
campion, alyssum, helianthus, lavender, and others
    which
You in Your infinite wisdom know are drought-
    loving plants—
I will write their names on a bit of paper if You
    like—
and grant that the sun may shine the whole day
    long,
but not everywhere (not, for instance, on the
    spiraea, or
on gentian, plantain lily, and rhododendron)
and not too much;
that there may be plenty of dew and little wind,
enough worms, no plant lice and snails,
no mildew, and that once a week thin liquid
    manure and guano
may fall from heaven.
Amen.

Karel Čapek

Appendix 1
Some Gardening Words Explained

Listed here for quick reference are a few of the most
frequently used gardening words.

ACID OR ALKALINE SOILS
Soil is referred to as alkaline or "sweet" when its degree of
pH is more than 7. It is acid or "sour" when this is below
7. The acidity and alkalinity varies with the chemical
composition of the soil and affects the plant's ability to
make use of the available nutrients there.

ANNUALS
Annuals are flowering plants which take less than one year
to complete their full life cycle (seed, through to flowering,
seed production, and then death). It is occasionally
practical to treat nonhardy perennials as if they were
annuals by permitting them to remain outside after the
summer and die there during the winter.

ANTIDESICCANTS
These are chemicals used to prevent loss of water from
leaves.

B & B STOCK
This refers to freshly dug plants wherein the ball of roots,
including the original surrounding soil, is wrapped in
burlap and then secured with heavy cord.

BARE-ROOT STOCK
Freshly dug plants, whose fine feeder roots and surrounding
original soil have been completely removed, are known as
bare-root stock.

BIENNIAL
Biennials are plants that take 2 years in which to complete their full life cycle; flowering and fruiting occurs in the second year.

BONSAI (pronounced bone-sigh)
This is a Japanese word which refers to the art of dwarfing trees and shrubs and maintaining them in shallow containers. Although the idea originated in China, the Japanese have developed the practice to the level with which Westerners are familiar.

BROADLEAVED EVERGREEN
This refers to a plant which retains a set of *leaves* (as differentiated from *needles*) throughout the year.

BULB
A bulb consists of a much shortened stem usually surrounded by modified fleshy leaves and buds. It contains the future flower's parts and food enough for a single growing period. Flowers grown from bulb may also be grown from seed but the process invariably takes some years. An example of a bulb is a tulip.

COMPOST AND COMPOST PILE
Compost is a mixture consisting of decomposed organic matter and is used for fertilizer and soil improvement. A compost pile may be composed of numerous "refuse" items and include leaves, weeds, plants, organic household garbage, animal manures, etc. Lime and other minerals may also be added. The pile should be several feet in size and normally requires several seasons to develop properly for effective garden use.

CONIFEROUS
Plants which bear true cones are called coniferous. Most of these are also evergreens, e.g. pines, junipers, etc.

CORM
This is a bulb-like, swollen, usually underground stem which has scale-like leaves and buds. An example of a corm is a crocus.

CULTIVATION
The loosening and reworking of the soil is known as cultivation.

CUTTINGS
This word refers to the parts of a plant (leaves or stems) which are induced to grow roots and give rise to new plants. It is a simple, often used method of propagation.

DAMPING OFF
This refers to a fungal disease which attacks seedlings, causing them to rot (and usually die).

DECIDUOUS PLANTS
Deciduous plants are those which shed all their leaves during the period they are resting or "dormant."

DORMANCY OR DORMANT PERIOD
Dormancy is a resting time for plants, similar to the hibernation of animals, during which the life processes are slowed down. Most plants have a definite period of rest but, depending on the species and environment, they may or may not lose their leaves.

ESPALIER
This is the bending, pruning, and training of flexible branches of trees and shrubs to grow flat against a form. The pattern is often symmetrical in design.

EVERGREEN
Any plant which retains its leaves or needles all year is an "evergreen." This word does *not* refer only to Christmas trees!

FLAT
A shallow pan in which seeds and young plants are started.

FOLIAR FEEDING
Foliar feeding is the spraying of certain water-soluble fertilizers directly onto the leaves of plants.

FRUIT
The fruit of a plant is that part (the ovary) which holds the seeds.

GENUS
A term used in plant classification, genus refers to a subdivision of a plant family. A genus may include one or more species. In botanical nomenclature the first name is the genus. An example would be the botanical name for the Firethorn, which is *Pyracantha coccinea*. "Pyracantha" is the genus.

HARDY PLANTS
The word "hardy" is used to describe plants which are able to survive local cold-weather conditions.

HERBACEOUS OR HERB
A plant which has a nonwoody stem is called herbaceous.

HUMUS
Incompletely decayed vegetable matter (with or without animal substance) which adds richness to the soil is known as humus.

LEGGY PLANTS
A plant which has lost all of its bottom leaves and is bare on its lower portions is called "leggy."

LOAM
"Loamy" is a description of a soil texture which is neither too heavy nor too loose and contains a suitable proportion of humus. It is considered the ideal planting medium for most plants.

MULCH
A mulch is protective covering placed on the ground around plants which helps to conserve moisture, inhibit weeds, reduce caking of the surface, and insulate against severe cold. A natural mulch, such as that found in forests, is composed of the dropped leaves and needles of the trees. In the garden virtually any material may qualify as a mulch.

ORGANIC GARDENING
This refers to a type of gardening in which only natural animal, vegetable, or mineral materials are used for fertilizer and soil improvement. Chemical insecticides are also avoided. An early advocate of purely organic gardening methods in the United States was J. I. Rodale. His extensive writings have influenced many.

PERENNIAL
A plant which lives from year to year, not dying after flowering, is called a perennial. While the word could be applied to all woody plants, it is used primarily to differentiate herbaceous ones from annuals and biennials.

pH
Used by gardeners when referring to the degree of acidity
or alkalinity of soil, pH is the universal symbol for the
hydrogen ion concentration. The pH value of the soil is
measured by a scale ranging from 1, which is most acid, up
to 14, which is most alkaline. Neutral is 7. Its limits of
importance to gardeners are between 4 and 9. The pH
degree varies with the chemical composition and the
physical structure of the soil.

POTBOUND
This term is used to describe a plant's root system which
has completely filled its container.

PROPAGATION
This is the reproduction of new plants from existing ones.
It consists of two basic categories: reproduction from seeds
(or spores) or reproduction by vegetative methods. One
vegetative method is by cuttings.

RHIZOME
This is an underground stem which grows horizontally and
is root-like in appearance. An example of a plant which
grows this way is the iris.

SELF-SOW
Seeds which have dropped from the parent plant and which
sprout by themselves where they have fallen are said to be
self-sown.

SEMI-EVERGREEN
A tree or shrub which holds many of its leaves through
most of the winter is referred to as semi-evergreen for the
locale.

SHRUB
This is a woody plant with several stems growing from the
ground or base.

SPECIES
Species is a term used in plant classification referring to a
group of plants considered to be closely related to each
other. In botanical nomenclature the second name is the
species. An example is the botanical name for the Firethorn,
which is *Pyracantha coccinea*. "coccinea" is the species.

SPECIMEN PLANT

This refers to a plant which is particularly unusual or well formed. Specimen trees or shrubs are often used as focal points in large gardens.

TENDER PLANTS

Plants which are unable to withstand severe or local cold-weather conditions are referred to as "tender" for the area.

VARIETY

This is a term used in plant classification referring to a plant placed in a *subdivision* of a species. It is usually represented in botanical nomenclature as the third name. An example is the botanical name for a variety of Firethorn, *Pyracantha coccinea lalandi.* "lalandi" is the variety name.

VINE

A vine is a climbing plant which must be supplied with a support for upright growth. Some vines have twining stems (clockwise or counterclockwise), others have tendrils, while still others send out tiny rootlets which adhere to the support.

WHIP

This refers to a very young, single-stemmed, unbranched woody plant.

WINTERKILL OR DIE-BACK

Varying degrees of damage may be incurred by plants because of severe winter temperature and winds. These words are used to describe the damage which may be confined to the tips or the entire top of the plant, and sometimes to the roots as well.

Appendix 2
Horticultural Organizations and Institutions for Extra Help

The following are open to the general public for membership, publish informative periodicals, and provide services and programs. Residence in the vicinity is not a prerequisite for membership.

THE AMERICAN HORTICULTURAL SOCIETY
publishes: *American Horticulturist News & Views* (bimonthly)
Mount Vernon, Va. 22121

ARNOLD ARBORETUM
publishes: *Arnoldia* (bimonthly)
Journal of the Arnold Arboretum (quarterly)
The Arborway
Jamaica Plain, Mass. 02130

BROOKLYN BOTANIC GARDEN
publishes: *Plants and Gardens* (quarterly)
1000 Washington Avenue
Brooklyn, N.Y. 11225

CALIFORNIA ARBORETUM FOUNDATION, INC.
publishes: *Lasca Leaves* (quarterly)
301 N. Baldwin Avenue
Arcadia, Calif. 91006

CHICAGO HORTICULTURAL SOCIETY & BOTANIC GARDEN
publishes: *Garden Talk* (bimonthly)
18 S. Michigan Avenue, Room 600
Chicago, Ill. 60603

CORNELL PLANTATIONS
publishes: *The Cornell Plantations* (quarterly)
100 Judd Falls Road
Ithaca, N.Y. 14850

DENVER BOTANIC GARDENS
publishes: *The Green Thumb* (quarterly)
Green Thumb Newsletter (monthly)
909 York Street
Denver, Colo. 80206

DESERT BOTANICAL GARDEN OF ARIZONA
publishes: *Saguaroland Bulletin* (10 times/yr.)
6400 E. McDowell Road
Box 5415
Phoenix, Ariz. 85010

FAIRCHILD TROPICAL GARDEN
publishes: *Fairchild Tropical Garden Bulletin* (quarterly)
10901 Old Cutler Road
Miami, Fla. 33156

THE GARDEN CENTER OF GREATER CLEVELAND
publishes: *The Garden Center Bulletin* (monthly)
11030 E. Boulevard
Cleveland, Ohio 44106

THE HOLDEN ARBORETUM
publishes: *Arboretum Leaves* (quarterly)
9500 Sperry Road
Mentor, Ohio 44060

HORTICULTURAL SOCIETY OF NEW YORK
publishes: *The Bulletin* (bimonthly)
128 W. 58 Street
New York, N.Y. 10019

MASSACHUSETTS HORTICULTURAL SOCIETY
publishes: *Horticulture* (monthly)
Nasturtium (monthly newsletter)
300 Massachusetts Ave.
Boston, Mass. 02115

MISSOURI BOTANICAL GARDEN
publishes: *Missouri Botanical Garden Bulletin* (bimonthly)
2315 Tower Grove Avenue
St. Louis, Mo. 63110

THE NEW YORK BOTANICAL GARDEN
publishes: *Garden Journal* (bimonthly)
Newsletter (monthly)
Bronx Park
Bronx, N.Y. 10458

NORFOLK BOTANICAL GARDEN SOCIETY
publishes: *Norfolk Botanical Garden Society Bulletin*
(monthly)
Airport Road
Norfolk, Va. 23518

THE PENNSYLVANIA HORTICULTURAL SOCIETY, INC.
publishes: *PHS News* (monthly)
Gardeners Guide (annually)
The Greene Scene (bimonthly)
Independence National Historical Park
325 Walnut Street
Philadelphia, Pa. 19106

QUEENS BOTANICAL GARDEN SOCIETY, INC.
publishes: *Gardens on Parade* (quarterly)
43–50 Main Street
Flushing, N.Y. 11355

STRYBING ARBORETUM SOCIETY OF GOLDEN GATE PARK
publishes: *Notes from Strybing Arboretum* (quarterly)
Hall of Flowers
Ninth Avenue and Lincoln Way
San Francisco, Calif. 94122

TENNESSEE BOTANICAL GARDENS AND FINE ARTS CENTER
publishes: *Cheekwood Mirror* (monthly)
Cheekwood
Cheek Road
Nashville, Tenn. 37205

TULSA GARDEN CENTER AND ROSE GARDENS
publishes: *Yearly Roster*
Monthly Bulletin
2435 S. Peoria Avenue
Tulsa, Okla. 74114

FRIENDS OF THE UNIVERSITY OF WASHINGTON ARBORETUM
College of Forest Resources
University of Washington
Seattle, Wash. 98105

UNITED STATES DEPARTMENT OF AGRICULTURE
publishes: *Home & Garden Bulletins*
(Complete catalog of many useful bulletins.
Price range—10¢ and up each)
U. S. Government Printing Office
Washington, D.C. 20402

AGRICULTURAL EXTENSION SERVICE
Providing services like soil tests and recommendations for
general plant procedures, this Service was described in the
Directory of American Horticulture as "the most extensive
and most readily available source of information." And it is.
The best way to find the county agent nearest you is in the
phone book under a Government listing "Agricultural
Agent" or "Extension Service." Or write your *State
University* and its *Department of Agricultural Information*.

For example, in New York State the address is:
Director of Cooperative Extension
N.Y.S. College of Agriculture
Cornell University
Ithaca, N.Y. 14850

Appendix 3
National Conservation Organizations

Membership in the following is open to all.

FRIENDS OF THE EARTH
publishes: *Not Man Apart*
529 Commercial Street
San Francisco, Calif. 94111

THE IZAAK WALTON LEAGUE OF AMERICA
publishes: *Outdoor America*
1326 Waukegan Road
Glenview, Ill. 60025

NATIONAL AUDUBON SOCIETY
publishes: *Audubon Magazine*
950 Third Avenue
New York, N.Y. 10022

NATIONAL WILDLIFE FEDERATION
publishes: *Conservation News*
Ranger Rick's Nature Magazine (for children)
1412 16th Street, N.W.
Washington, D.C. 20036

THE NATURE CONSERVANCY
publishes: *The Nature Conservancy News*
Suite 800
1800 N. Kent Street
Arlington, Va. 22209

SIERRA CLUB
publishes: *Sierra Club Bulletin*
National News Report
1050 Mills Tower
San Francisco, Calif. 94104

THE WILDERNESS SOCIETY
publishes: *The Living Wilderness*
1901 Pennsylvania Avenue, N.W.
Washington, D.C. 20006

Selected Bibliography and Suggested Reading

This is a list of some of the works used in preparing this book.
It should suffice for those wishing to delve further into a particular subject.

GARDENING BOOKS:

Argall, Phyllis
DWARF TREES IN THE JAPANESE MODE
New York: The Citadel Press, 1964

Askwith, H.
THE COMPLETE GUIDE TO GARDEN FLOWERS
New York: A. S. Barnes, 1961

Baumgardt, J. P.
HOW TO PRUNE ALMOST EVERYTHING
New York: William Morrow & Co., 1968

Borror, Donald J. and White, R. E.
A FIELD GUIDE TO THE INSECTS OF AMERICA NORTH OF MEXICO
Boston: Houghton Mifflin Co., 1970

Donahue, Roy L.
SOILS, AN INTRODUCTION TO SOILS AND PLANT GROWTH
Englewood Cliffs, N.J.: Prentice-Hall, Inc, 1958

Edinger, Philip
HOW TO GROW HERBS
Menlo Park, Calif.: A Sunset Book, Lane Magazine & Book Co., 1973

Everett, T. H.
NEW ILLUSTRATED ENCYCLOPEDIA OF GARDENING
New York: Greystone Press, 1967

Field, Xenia
WINDOW-BOX GARDENING
London: Studio Vista Ltd., 1965

Fox, Helen M.
GARDENING WITH HERBS
New York: Sterling Publishing Co., 1970
Free, Montague
GARDENING: A COMPLETE GUIDE TO
GARDEN MAKING
New York: Harcourt, Brace & Co., 1937
PLANT PRUNING IN PICTURES
Garden City, N.Y.: Doubleday & Co., American
Garden Guild, 1961
Gomez, N.
YOUR GARDEN IN THE CITY
New York: Oxford University Press, 1941
Grabe, A. V.
COMPLETE BOOK OF HOUSE PLANTS
New York: Random House, 1958
Hay, R. and Synge, P. M.
THE COLOR DICTIONARY OF FLOWERS
& PLANTS FOR HOME & GARDEN
New York: Crown Publishers, Inc., 1969
Hottes, A. C.
THE BOOK OF SHRUBS
New York: A. T. DeLaMare Co., Inc., 1928
Hunter, Beatrice T.
GARDENING WITHOUT POISONS
Boston: Houghton Mifflin Co., 1971
Kellogg, Charles E.
OUR GARDEN SOILS
New York: The Macmillan Co., 1952
Kressy, Michael
HOW TO GROW YOUR OWN VEGETABLES
Des Moines, Iowa: Creative Home Library, 1973
McDowell, Jack (editor)
BONSAI CULTURE AND CARE OF
MINIATURE TREES
Menlo Park, Calif.: A Sunset
Book, Lane Books, 1972
Mellon, I.
ROOF GARDENING
New York: A. T. DeLaMare Co., 1929
Moore, S. B.
ORNAMENTAL HORTICULTURE AS A
VOCATION
Fairborn, Ohio: Mor-Mac Publishing Co., 1969
Morse, H. K.
GARDENING IN THE SHADE
New York: Charles Scribner's Sons, 1962

Nehrling, A. and I.
THE PICTURE BOOK OF PERENNIALS
New York: Hearthside Press, Inc., 1964

Ortloff, H. S. and Raymore, H. B.
A BOOK ABOUT SOILS FOR THE HOME
GARDENER
New York: M. Barrows & Co., Inc., 1962

Pirone, Pascal P.
DISEASES AND PESTS OF ORNAMENTAL
PLANTS
New York: Ronald Press, 1970

Rodale, J. I.
PAY DIRT
New York: The Devin-Adair Co., 1950

Rodale, Robert [and others] (editors)
THE ORGANIC WAY TO MULCHING
Emmaus, Pa.: Rodale Press, 1972

Shurtleff, M.
HOW TO CONTROL PLANT DISEASES
Ames, Iowa: Iowa State University Press, 1966

Sunset Editors
GARDENING IN CONTAINERS
Menlo Park, Calif.: A Sunset Book, Lane Books,
1969

Taylor, N.
TAYLOR'S ENCYCLOPEDIA OF GARDENING
Boston: Houghton Mifflin Co., 1961

Truex, Philip
THE CITY GARDENER
New York: Alfred A. Knopf, 1964

Tyler, H.
ORGANIC GARDENING WITHOUT
POISONS
New York: Van Nostrand-Reinhold Co., 1970

Vivian, A.
FIRST PRINCIPLES OF SOIL FERTILITY
New York: Orange Judd Publishing Co., 1923

Westcott, Cynthia
ARE YOU YOUR GARDEN'S WORST PEST?
Garden City, N.Y.: Doubleday & Co., Inc., 1961

PLANT DISEASE HANDBOOK
New York: Van Nostrand-Reinhold Co., 1971

THE GARDENER'S BUG BOOK
Garden City, N.Y.: Doubleday & Co., Inc., 1964

White, M. G.
    POTS AND POT GARDENS
    London: Abelard-Schuman, 1969
Yoshimura, Yuji and Halford, Giovanna M.
    THE JAPANESE ART OF MINIATURE TREES
    AND LANDSCAPES
    Rutland, Vt., and Tokyo: Charles E. Tuttle Co.,
    1971
Zion, R. L.
    TREES FOR ARCHITECTURE AND THE
    LANDSCAPE
    New York: Reinhold Book Corp., 1968

GARDENING PERIODICALS:

PLANTS & GARDENS HANDBOOK SERIES
New York: Brooklyn Botanic Garden
    Epstein, Harold (editor)
        GARDENING IN THE SHADE
        Vol. 25, no. 3
    Frese, Paul F. (editor)
        PRUNING HANDBOOK
        Vol. 14, no. 3
    Harkness, Bernard (editor)
        HANDBOOK ON FLOWERING SHRUBS
        Vol. 20, no. 1
    Lunt, H. A. (editor)
        HANDBOOK ON SOILS
        Vol. 12, no. 1
    Nehrling, A. and I. (editors)
        SUMMER FLOWERS FOR CONTINUING
        BLOOM
        Vol. 24, no. 1
    Nelson, P. K. and Wyman, D. (editors)
        HANDBOOK ON VINES
        Vol. 10, no. 1
    Teuscher, Henry (editor)
        GARDENING IN CONTAINERS
        Vol. 14, no. 1
    Westcott, Cynthia (editor)
        HANDBOOK ON BIOLOGICAL CONTROL
        OF PLANT PESTS
        Vol. 16, no. 3

Westcott, Cynthia and Walker, J. T.
(editors)
HANDBOOK ON GARDEN PESTS
Vol. 22, no. 1
Yashiroda, K. (editor)
BONSAI, SPECIAL TECHNIQUES
Vol. 22, no. 2
HANDBOOK ON DWARFED POTTED
TREES, The Bonsai of Japan
Vol. 9, no. 3

CONTROL GARDEN PESTS WITHOUT POISON
SPRAYS
Emmaus, Pa.: Rodale Press, J. I. Rodale
(editor), 1965
CORNELL RECOMMENDATIONS FOR
COMMERCIAL FLORICULTURE CROPS
Ithaca, N.Y.: N.Y.S. College of Agriculture, 1971
DIRECTORY OF AMERICAN HORTICULTURE
Mount Vernon, Va.: The American Horticultural
Society, Inc., 1972
GARDEN JOURNAL
Bronx: The New York Botanical Garden,
Mary E. O'Brien (editor). Misc. issues
HORTICULTURE
Boston: Massachusetts Horticultural Society, E. F.
Steffek (editor). Misc. issues
NEWSLETTER
East Norwich, L.I., N.Y.: Martin Viette Nurseries,
Andre and Claire Viette (editors). Misc. issues
ORGANIC GARDENING AND FARMING
Emmaus, Pa.: Rodale Press, Inc., R. Rodale
(editor). Misc. issues
ORTHO LAWN & GARDEN BOOKS
San Francisco: Chevron Chemical Co.
Misc. issues
THE BEST GARDENING IDEAS I KNOW
Emmaus, Pa.: Rodale Press, Inc., J. I. Rodale (editor)
UNITED STATES DEPARTMENT OF
AGRICULTURE (USDA)
Washington, D.C.: United States
Government Printing Office. Misc. bulletins

Index

87–88, 90, 107, 197 (fotos)
62–63 (list)
Propagation, 255
Pruning
  bonsai influence on, 199
  as compensation for root loss, 227
  for disease or pest control, 153, 201
  how to do, 200 (dwg)
  reasons for, 200–4
  tools for, 211–12
  when to do, 204–6
Pruning of roots. See Root pruning
Prunus amygdalus. See Flowering
  almond
Prunus cerasifera. See Purple leaf
  plum
Prunus serrulata. See Flowering
  cherry
Purple leaf plum, 62–63 (list)
Pussy willow, 62–63 (list)
Pyracantha coccinea. See Firethorn
Pyrethrum, 166
Pyrus calleryana. See Callery pear

R

Rain
  in covered planting areas, 31–32
  insufficiency of, in winter, 139
  gage, 143, 145 (foto)
Ra-pid-Gro, 218
Redbud, 64–65 (list)
Reflected light, 24, 26
Rhizome, 255
Rhododendron
  as a poisonous plant, 84
  92, 93, 109 (fotos)
  64–65 (list)
Rock phosphate, 222
Rodale, J. I., 189
Roof. See Covered planting areas
Root pruning
  bonsai methods of, 224–25
  in the established garden, 224–26
  in the fall, 191
  237 (fotos)
Roots. See also Root pruning
  of B & B stock, 4
  burned by sun, 132–33

drainage around, 114, 134
in nursery containers, 5
rot or knots, 177 (dwg)
of sick plants, 176, 178
of wild plants, 15
winter damaged, 95
Rose. See also Climbing roses
  bud with aphids, 180 (foto)
  in cardboard nursery containers,
    121, 127 (foto)
  shrub, 64–65 (list)
  standard, 40 (foto)
  23 (dwg)
  86 (foto)
Rose mallow, 64–65 (list)
Rosenwach Water Tank Co., 101
Rose of Sharon. See Rose mallow
Rotenone, 166
Rozen, Dr. Jerome, Jr., 243
Rudbeckia, 82 (list)
Russian olive
  214 (foto)
  64–65 (list)
Rust, 98, 101

S

Safe insect controls, 151–54
Saffer, Al & Co., 99, 142
Salix. See Weeping willow
Salix discolor. See Pussy willow
Salpiglossis, 82 (list)
Salvia, 82 (list)
Sand, 113
Sanitation
  fall cleanup, 188
    for disease control, 170
    for pest control, 152
    tool disinfecting, 170
Scale, 158
  162 (dwg)
  181 (fotos)
Science systemic, 165
Scion, 203
Scorch, 171
Sculpture, 36
  43, 107 (fotos)
Seasons, 29. See also Lists of plant
  names
  almanac for work during, 234

Farewell! Like a bee
reluctant to leave the deeps
of a peony.
                              Basho